Tennyson
and
Tradition

Tennyson
and
Tradition

Robert Pattison

HARVARD UNIVERSITY PRESS
Cambridge, Massachusetts
and London, England 1979

Copyright © 1979 by the President and Fellows of Harvard College
All rights reserved
Printed in the United States of America
Publication of this book has been aided by a grant from the
Andrew W. Mellon Foundation.

Library of Congress Cataloging in Publication Data

Pattison, Robert.
 Tennyson and tradition.

 Includes bibliographical references and index.
 1. Tennyson, Alfred Tennyson, Baron, 1809–1892—
Criticism and interpretation.   2. Pastoral poetry—
History and criticism.   I. Title.
PB5588.P37   821'.8   79–13247
ISBN 0–674–87415–3

In memory of
Charles Kerr
1945–1979

Acknowledgments

ANYONE who writes about Alfred Tennyson owes a huge debt to Christopher Ricks's edition of the poetry (1969), as well as his life of Tennyson (1972), both of which are monuments of Victorian studies. In this book all quotations from Tennyson follow Ricks's edition in spelling, punctuation, and line numbers. The dates given for poems are those of publication. Four other recent books have also influenced me beyond the limits of the usual scholarly apparatus to acknowledge: A. Dwight Culler, *The Poetry of Tennyson* (1977); James R. Kincaid, *Tennyson's Major Poems: The Comic and Ironic Patterns* (1975); F. E. L. Priestley, *Language and Structure in Tennyson's Poetry* (1973); and John D. Rosenberg, *The Fall of Camelot* (1973). A book such as this usually takes note of other critics only to refine or refute their arguments; my disagreements with these authors are slight by comparison with the thanks I owe them.

I am very grateful to Alan Shaw and Curtis Church for their advice and help on the manuscript.

Contents

ONE

Tennyson and the Uses of Tradition

TENNYSON, who brooded on universal process as few poets have, exhibits in his development of the poetic tradition and its genres a paradigm of process. Rightly understood, Tennyson's use of tradition provides a diagram of his mind. It is the aim of this study to define the forms Tennyson used, show why he chose to work with them, and demonstrate how he evolved these forms in a manner that accorded with his poetic vision. If the book helps elevate Tennyson's reputation as a craftsman consciously working within a long and complex tradition of poetic forms, it will have done its job. If, secondarily, it illuminates the extent to which critical theory, usually considered the Victorians' weak suit, was in fact an active force among them, at least in the work of their greatest poet, it will have served Tennyson and his period well.

There is now, I hope, general agreement that Tennyson was more than a mindless artificer of lovely expressions. I shall treat him, as I think he would have wished, as a man wholly absorbed in the profession of poetry, who exercised a zealous but playful dominion over the poetic craft and tradition. That he was in fact wholly absorbed in the craft of poetry—its meters, forms, conventions, rhythms—is attested by the voluminous records of his daily life and conversations: by twelve he was producing adaptations of the classics in heroic couplets, and from an early age his table talk drifted instinctively to discussions of metrics. Neither interest ever left him; the Homeric translations written in 1863 are only the most obvious example of a passion for adapting the tradition into English verse, which pervades all his poetry, and his preoccupation with meters, both ancient and modern, stifled more than one dinner party: William Allingham describes a visit to Farringford in 1863 during which the dinner talk for three nights running was Sapphics and Anacreontics; on the third night, "Mrs. Tennyson confessed herself tired of hearing about 'Classical Metres.' "[1] Not even the most devout attendants of the bard could tolerate his full infatuation with the poetic calling, but he himself seems to have derived vital sustenance from his immersion in the craft of poetry, and in the last months of his life, his health failing, he could still be rallied by a discussion of the virtues of Gray's *Elegy* or the vanity of French Alexandrines.[2]

While the craft sustained him, however, the tradition of poetry simultaneously stimulated and vexed him: "Blessed, cursed, Memory," he wrote in *Memory* early in his career. It is a paradox that appears throughout his early verse: the past is at once a weight suppressing the craftsman's creativity and the wellspring of the craft itself. Critics have been too ready to find in Tennyson's poetry only the weight of the tradition, the cursed and not the blessed aspect of cultural memory; thus his work is often read as an imitation or translation of a tradition from which he saw no escape. This criticism takes both its most flattering and its most insidious form in the venerable comparison between Vergil and Tennyson,[3] a double-edged compliment carrying the implication that the Victorian bard was but an echo of the tradition, and not an improvement upon it.

No one was more conscious of this criticism than Tennyson himself, and he took considerable pains to meet it in his verse. His poem *To Virgil* (1882) is certainly full of Vergilian echoes, and yet it is couched not in the heroic dactyl but in the trochee, a meter that Tennyson had made his own vehicle. The process is typical of Tennyson's approach to the tradition: to use it as a source out of which the craftsman evolves new creations, creations that are demonstrably linked to tradition but surpass it. If Tennyson is in fact another Vergil, he is so because he treats his sources in the same way the Roman poet treats his: as the evidences of a plastic tradition to be evolved through the cultural process of poetry. The author of the *Aeneid* ransacked ancient culture to produce a distinct and wholly original epitome of the world as he saw it. Tennyson used the tradition in exactly this Vergilian way.

Thus for him "Blessed, cursed, Memory" is literally and very significantly the mother of the Muses, especially the poetic Muses, for it is through the memory of the entire tradition of poetry that the poet is supplied with his materials:

> Thou who stealest fire,
> From the fountains of the past,
> To glorify the present; oh, haste,
> Visit my low desire!
> Strengthen me, enlighten me!
> I faint in this obscurity,
> Thou dewy dawn of memory.   (1–7)

This is Tennyson in his very early *Ode to Memory*, announcing a credo that will animate his whole work: the craft of the latter-day poet lies in his manipulation of tradition and not in any completely original departure, which would be an impossibility since the great innovations, which Mnemosyne cherishes with special zeal, lie in the cultural past:

> For the discovery
> And newness of thine art so pleased thee,
> That all which thou hast drawn of fairest
> Or boldest since, but lightly weighs
> With thee unto the love thou bearest
> The first-born of thy genius. Artist-like,
> Ever retiring thou dost gaze
> On the prime labour of thine early days.   (87–94)

But if Memory admonishes the poet that true innovations are in his culture's past, she also provides access to the spirit and forms of poetic creativity, and inspired by her,

> We may hold converse with all forms
> Of the many-sided mind,
> And those whom passion hath not blinded,
> Subtle-thoughted, myriad-minded. (114–118)

The forms of the past are the key to the many-sided mind of man, and both these forms and the humanity they represent are the proper studies of the poet, whose latter-day role is not that of a discoverer or innovator, but that of the "subtle-thoughted, myriad-minded" craftsman. Thus the way to an understanding of "Universal Nature moved by Universal Mind," the poetic achievement Tennyson attributed to his epic predecessor in *To Virgil* and consciously strove to emulate, lies not through simple imitation of the tradition, but through the study and manipulation of the forms in which mind has expressed itself. To these forms Memory holds the key.

The *Ode to Memory* was written before the poet was twenty, and probably as early as 1825, yet its sentiments remained with Tennyson throughout his life, and some sixty years later the same thought was restated in one of his last poems, *Akbar's Dream:*

> And what are forms?
> Fair garments, plain or rich, and fitting close
> Or flying looselier, warmed but by the heart
> Within them, moved but by the living limb,
> And cast aside, when old, for newer, —Forms!
> The Spiritual in Nature's market-place—
> The silent Alphabet-of-heaven-in-man
> Made vocal—banners blazoning a Power
> That is not seen and rules from far away—
> A silken cord let down from Paradise,
> When fine philosophies would fail, to draw
> The crowd from wallowing in the mire of earth,
> And all the more, when these behold their Lord,
> Who shaped the forms, obey them, and himself
> Here on this bank in *some* way live the life
> Beyond the bridge, and serve that Infinite
> Within us, as without, that All-in-all,
> And over-all, the never-changing One
> And ever-changing Many. (123–140)

The forms are the manifestation of the infinite, granted to man as a dispensation when "philosophies would fail," by which he is permitted to comprehend "that Infinite / Within us." Tennyson had good reason to be attracked by Akbar, for just as the Mogul potentate had sought to find the best and the universal in all the religious forms practiced by his subjects, so Tennyson searched for the truest and most enduring elements in the poetic tradition. And as Akbar had hoped to fashion from the various religious forms adopted by his subjects a single true faith that transcended them all by incorporating them all, so Tennyson aimed to fashion a new poetic out of the inherited forms of Western culture, a poetic more truly expressive of the Universal Mind, which he believed was but imperfectly expressed in the distinct and individual forms of the tradition.

That Tennyson did in fact manipulate the poetic tradition will seem to many a dubious proposition. There is no dispute that he used it; a glance at any page of Christopher Ricks's edition of the complete poetry will provide a sample of the parallel references it is possible to adduce between Tennyson and every poet from Homer up to Moore. But on the whole Tennyson has been regarded merely as a borrower, and the quantity of his borrowings has tended to obscure the artistry with which they were deployed—a critical lapse that annoyed no one more than Tennyson himself, for the charge that Tennyson was a translator more than an artist was made late in his lifetime by John Churton Collins.

"Collins," boomed Tennyson, "is a louse upon the locks of scholarship."[4] Collins was a professor of English and a literary critic, whose specialty was discovering parallels between texts, usually in the form of verbal allusions or echoes. He had, in 1880 and 1881, published a series of articles in the *Cornhill* magazine describing Tennyson as among that "class of poets who are essentially imitative and reflective. The poets of Alexandria, the epic and elegiac poets of Rome, are the most striking types of this class in ancient times. Torquato Tasso, Gray, and Mr. Tennyson are, perhaps, the most striking types in the modern world."[5] Following this initial assertion, he cited a dizzying succession of instances in which he felt Tennyson had recalled ancient and modern authors in formulating his verse. As the tone of Collins's articles and books was uniformly flattering to the bard, Tennyson could not have objected to any malice in the critic. Indeed, while Tennyson possessed in abundance what Alfred Austin called "literary sensitiveness,"[6] he bore no grudge toward his detractors. Even John Wilson, who as "Christopher North" had written one review and suborned another that, taken together, severely damaged the sale of Tennyson's early publications (1830, 1832), received a frank and even kind letter from Tennyson, and many who had been critics were Tennyson's frequent guests. Collins alone earned Tennyson's scorn; the poet mentioned Collins frequently in conversation, and always with contempt.[7]

Since the kind of source study in which Collins was engaged is a recognized field of scholarship, one that has often been applied to Tennyson's work (and will be again in this book), it is worthwhile to consider the exact grounds for Tennyson's objections to Collins's researches, the validity of those objections, and the best method by which to measure Tennyson's use of and reliance on earlier works.

This task is made easier by the survival of Tennyson's copy of the *Cornhill* containing the first of Collins's articles. In the margin, Tennyson made numerous notations on the accuracy of the parallels cited by the critic.[8] He dismissed most of Collins's echoes with a "no," a row of exclamation marks expressing consternation, or a monosyllabic rebuttal, as in the case of the laconic "oh" next to the citation of Shelley's "I change, but I cannot die" (*The Clouds* 76) in conjunction with

> Nothing will die;
> All things will change
> Through eternity.

Some parallels required several words of dismissal. Next to the suggestion that the line from *The Two Voices*, "You scarce could see the grass for flowers," is an imitation of George Peele's "Ye may ne see for peeping flowers the grass," Tennyson wrote, "Made in the Fields." He was obviously piqued at being thought of as a poet who worked entirely from sources, not nature itself; this latent charge of artificiality in Collins's articles was in fact a primary cause of his indignation. In general Collins's cross-references are either so obvious or so fatuous (perhaps the most outrageous is the gloss of a line in *Locksley Hall* from three different parts of Plotinus' *Enneads*) that it is a marvel Tennyson expended so much effort on them.

Yet the obvious parallels, such as "This way and that dividing the swift mind" from the *Morte d'Arthur* with "atque animum nunc huc celerem, nunc dividit illuc" from the *Aeneid* (4.285), he admitted only grudgingly with a "granted," or a "possibly." In several cases he abjured knowledge of a source Collins cited, only to cite the same source himself in later editions of his works. One such line is "For now the noonday quiet holds the hill" from *Oenone*, which he glossed with a reference to Callimachus' *Lavacrum Palladis* (72). When Collins had cited the same line in 1880, Tennyson had marked "not known to me" next to the reference. A similar instance of Tennyson's denying a borrowing is the marginal note in his copy of F. J. Rowe and W. T. Webb's *Selections* (1888) next to the citation of Claudian's "venerandus apex et cognita cunctis canities" in conjunction with "O good gray head which all men knew" from the *Ode on the Death of the Duke of Wellington*. Tennyson's note reads, "never heard of Claudian's line!" This is surprising, since he had translated a portion of Claudian before he was fourteen and must have been intimate with his work.

Perhaps Tennyson's comments only prove the New Critical maxim that authors make poor commentators on their own texts; but his indignation with Collins, if it sheds curious light on the poet's use of sources, reveals the area of craftsmanship about which he was touchiest—his originality. At first glance, his sensitiveness on this point will seem the more extraordinary because Collins and the others who have studied Tennyson in terms of verbal echoes and parallels are clearly correct: he is par excellence a poet of borrowings. Some of his poems, such as *Oenone* or *Lucretius*, are almost pastiches of classical quotations, most of which were advertised by Tennyson himself in the notes he wrote to accompany later editions. Why, then, Tennyson's extreme reaction to the sort of criticism Collins practiced?

The answer is that Collins's approach to Tennyson was based on a dangerous half-truth, one which has lingered on in Tennyson studies. Tennyson was an even greater borrower than Milton, as a century of criticism has shown. This aspect of his poetry was as conscious as it had been with Vergil and Milton. What Tennyson objected to in Collins's approach was not this obvious premise, but the failure to go beyond the premise, a failure that resulted in the implication that Tennyson's work was in part a plagiarism, exactly the word the bard used to describe the charge he felt Collins had brought against his work.[9] Tennyson, one of the most tradition-bound of English poets, was deeply incensed by the charge that he was not original, more incensed than by any other criticism brought against him during all his years of following the critics. His anger with Collins actually amounted to an assertion of his creativity.

This mixture of creativity and borrowing, a familiar characteristic of seventeenth-century poetry, has often been mistaken for a form of translation in nineteenth-century texts, or worse, for a form of Alexandrian literary dressing. Tennyson would have despised either notion. Let us take *Mariana* (1830) as an early and indicative species of Tennyson's use of sources. Both Collins, in his *Cornhill* articles, and Christopher Ricks, in his edition of Tennyson's poetry, have suggested sources for and parallel passages to *Mariana*. Ricks believes the poem to have been heavily influenced by six writers: Keats, in *Isabella* (233–242), *Sleep and Poetry* (146), and *The Eve of St. Agnes* (49); Samuel Rogers, *Captivity*; Horace, *Odes* (2.9.10–12); Shakespeare, *Romeo and Juliet* (2.3.1, 5); Milton, *Lycidas* (97); and Vergil, *Aeneid* (4.451). To this already eclectic list can be added Collins's two citations: fragment 71 of the lyrics attributed to Sappho and Cinna's lines "Te matutinius flentem conspexit Eous, / Te flentem paulo vidit post Hesperus idem." Finally we can add Shakespeare's *Measure for Measure*, which Tennyson himself acknowledged, in the epigraph to the poem, "Mariana in the moated grange." Let us try, first, to determine which, if any, of these are genuine borrowings by Tennyson, and which are merely echoes that Tennyson might have dismissed with a no. Then, if we can determine the genuine borrowings, we may be able to find a pattern or method in their use.

In ascertaining the validity of these glosses we could rely on Tennyson's own estimation of various authors and the books we know he owned and read. This would prove to be a dubious method, however. For instance, Tennyson had a high regard for Keats's poetry and spoke of him in the loftiest terms. Late in his life Tennyson told Arthur Coleridge, "Keats would have become one of the very greatest of all poets, had he lived. At the time of his death there was apparently no sign of exhaustion or having written himself out." But liking and borrowing are two different things, and on another occasion Tennyson said, on being asked if Keats and Horace were his masters, "No, Keats and Horace were great masters. Not my masters!"[10] The poet may have forgotten in his old age how indebted his early volumes had been to Keats; or perhaps the critics have been wrong and the early poetry, *Mariana* included, was not so strongly influenced by Keats as has been believed. Tennyson's comments, then, cancel each other out and do not reveal whether Keats really was a source for *Mariana*.

The parallel with Keats's *Isabella* might be allowed because of its verbal likeness to *Mariana*, though even this is not very exact. A stronger argument for allowing it, however, would be that both poems deal with women who have lost their lovers, though Isabella's has been murdered and the text does not tell us what has become of Mariana's. (If she is literally Shakespeare's Mariana, she has been deserted.) Then the passages could be called parallel because they would have both a verbal and a contextual similarity, on which Tennyson is playing. This same approach would make sense of the echo of Vergil in the poem, "She could not look on the sweet heaven" (15), since the parallel passage in the *Aeneid*, "taedet caeli convexa tueri" ("she is weary with looking on the dome of heaven")[11] describes Dido deserted by Aeneas and praying, like Mariana, for death in the same lines: "Tum vero infelix exterrita Dido / mortem orat; taedit caeli convexa tueri" (4.450–451).

The echo of Cinna may be dismissed as invalid on Tennyson's own assertion, in his marginalia to Collins's *Cornhill* article, that he had never read the poem, even though this may be a risky authority.

The parallel with Horace is dubious, first, because his ode is verbally not very close to Tennyson's "Her tears fell with the dews at even; / Her tears fell ere the dews were dried" (12–15). Horace has

> nec tibi Vespero
> surgente decedunt amores
> nec rapidum fugiente solem

or roughly, "Your love ceases not with the rising evening star nor when it flees the swift sun," which is far from being an exact correlation of the texts. Second, the context of the two poems is very different; Horace's is a consolation ode addressed to his friend Valgius, and it lacks the sexual dimension that seems to have been the deciding factor in Tennyson's choice of sources for *Mariana*. On the other hand, Tennyson's use of Horace, and for that matter Cinna, might be vindicated, not in terms of the context in which they wrote but in reference to their lyric forms.

If we accept the idea that the sexual context was uppermost in Tennyson's mind, then we can also include the Samuel Rogers poem as a source. In his old age Tennyson could still recite it by heart and with admiration,[12] and more important, it has the same sort of sexual suggestiveness as the Tennyson piece, though in a less developed form.

> Caged in old woods, whose reverend echoes wake
> When the hern screams along the distant lake,
> Her little heart oft flutters to be free,
> Oft sighs to turn the unrelenting key.
> In vain! the nurse that rusted relic wears,
> Nor moved by gold—nor moved by tears;
> And terraced walls their black reflection throw
> On the green-mantled moat that sleeps below.

The isolation of the scene, the hint of sexuality grown old with waiting, and the detail of molds and algae to convey the image of captive desire, all are Tennysonian material, as is a vagueness of place and prisoner alike. This vagueness is essential to the working of *Mariana* because it is a poem about something very hard to localize: thwarted desire.

Collins's suggestion that *Mariana* was inspired by the four lines attributed to Sappho,

> Δέδυκε μὲν ἀ οελάννα
> και Πληΐαδες, μέσαι δὲ
> νύκτες, παρὰ δ' ἔρχεται ὦρα,
> ἔγω δε μόνα κατεύδω[13]

> The moon and the Pleiades are out; it is the middle of the
> night and hours pass; I fall asleep alone

seems much more probably than his Cinna parallel, for the Sapphic lines are suggestive of sexual anxiety and are also encapsulated in a kind of elliptical lyric statement that intrigued Tennyson and that he imitated in *Mariana*. We also know that Tennyson was a great admirer of Sappho; that in several of his early poems he glosses her influence (as in *Eleänore* and *Fatima*); and that Arthur Hallam felt the Sapphic fragments were especially akin to the later reworking of *Mariana* entitled *Mariana in the South*.[14] Against such evidence, Collins's parallel can hardly be dismissed. But it is important to realize that Tennyson did not use the Sapphic lyric simply because he liked it, but because it provided an appropriate lyric context upon which he could dilate, both in terms of form, for the brief lyric is vastly expanded in Tennyson's rendition, and of theme.

Tennyson seems to have consciously borrowed from works that had, like *Mariana*, a context of thwarted passion. Thus his glancing echo of *Romeo and Juliet* in the epithet "grey-eyed morn" is probably not accidental, and the borrowing of "Upon the middle of the night" from the scene in *Measure for Measure* (4.1.37), in which Isabella is discussing Mariana's coming tryst with Angelo, is a proper reference not only to the source from which Tennyson's heroine is derived, but to the sexual context in which he has placed her. The remaining parallels cited by Ricks, both to *Lycidas*, seem negligible: "wild winds bound within their cell" and "the day / Was sloping toward his western bower" are as much Homeric as they are Miltonic; they are expressions that belong to the common stock of Western poetry.

If we assume, then, that Tennyson was not merely a translator of admirable phrases from the classics but a conscious manipulator of his sources, we will be able to develop a workable rule for judging his borrowings. Echoes of earlier poems are probably just that—echoes—unless the original context of the borrowed material has some relation, either formal or thematic, to the context in which Tennyson used it. It will, of course, be useful to buttress this premise with evidence that Tennyson knew or admired the parallel text, but it seems more important critically, especially since Tennyson's recorded statements on what he knew and what he liked are often contradictory, to determine whether there is some artistic justification in the borrowing.[15] And of course, if Tennyson points out a source for his work, as he does in *Mariana* with the reference to *Measure for Measure*, special attention should be paid to it. Mariana is in fact a careful rendering of the Shakespearean character, whom Angelo "left in her tears" (3.1.233) and whose love has with rejection become "more violent and unruly" (3.1.253). More important, Mariana is the compromised character in an explicitly sexual drama who eagerly accepts the assignment from which the chaste Isabella recoils. Tennyson borrowed not only Mariana's moated grange, her tears, and her unruly passions, but also the entire milieu in which the original Mariana was figured; in Tennyson's poem she becomes what she only is by implication in the original—a character study of unrequited physical love. Thus her surroundings are acutely physical:

> The doors upon their hinges creaked;
> The blue fly sung in the pane; the mouse
> Behind the mouldering wainscot shrieked. (62–64)

When Millais painted Mariana in 1851, his color and detail rendered the sensual aspect of her emotion, and he positioned her in front of a stained-glass window in a pose that evokes a sexual interpretation. Millais's stained-glass window is an important, and an accurate, detail: by placing Mariana quite literally in a medieval light he suggests allegory, and this suggestion is faithful to Tennyson's text: the Mariana distilled from Shakespeare and presented with hints of Dido and of Rogers's captive lady is a universalized example of thwarted passion surrendered to the control of Thanatos.

More proof that Tennyson was working from a controlled group of sources to formulate highly refined models of emotional states in his early poems is found in his juxtaposition of *Mariana* and *Isabel* in all the editions of his poetry that he oversaw.[16] The source for both poems is *Measure for Measure*, and Isabel is a model of chastity in contrast to Mariana's withering sexuality. The characters are mirror images. Mariana is surrounded by black ("blackest moss," "blackened waters"), sunsets, decay, and images of small animal life (the fly, the mouse, the sparrow). Isabel is figured in terms of white or translucence:

> the clear-pointed flame of chastity,
> Clear, without heat, undying, tended by
> Pure vestal thoughts in the translucent fane
> Of her still spirit. (2–5)

While Mariana is pictured in terms of falling and setting, Isabel is surrounded by things upright ("A love still burning upward"), though in contrast to Mariana there is virtually nothing physical around Isabel; she is only described physically in terms of similes which "shadow forth" her goodness:

> A clear stream flowing with a muddy one,
> Till in its onward current it absorbs
> With swifter movement and in purer light
> The vexed eddies of its wayward brother. (30–33)

The simile, clearly derived from the plot of *Measure for Measure*, shadows Isabel forth; Mariana, on the other hand, does not cast but is covered by shadows:

> The shadow of the poplar fell
> Upon her bed, across her brow. (55–56)

These two early poems are obviously experimental. Both derive from a common source and seek to embody generalized concepts in female characters, and in each case the means of poetic expression is built around the personality of the subject. Isabel's chastity evokes the ode, traditionally reserved for grand or sublime topics, while Mariana is embedded in a specially designed stanza that is reminiscent of lyric and ballad structure and calls upon dramatic and epic sources as well. There is no question that *Mariana* is the greater poem, because the poetic devices by which Tennyson hoped to show that sensuality is decadent—the physical description, the narrative framework, Mariana's direct speech—give the poem an immediacy that the abstracted Isabel cannot possess. Tennyson in later life was in no doubt as to which of the two experimental methods was better for portraying universal subjects in the form of single characters—or as to which type of character, virtue or vice, was more evocative. Vivien and Guinevere are Mariana's direct descendants.

The pattern of source use established in these two experimental pieces holds good through most of Tennyson's works: the borrowings are not made randomly, or simply for their music, but are directly related to the formal and thematic context of the original as well as the new poem; the sources are not nearly so obscure as Collins, or even Ricks, would often have them (in *Mariana* we are dealing with Vergil, Shakespeare, Samuel Rogers, and perhaps Keats)— and Tennyson himself has provided the most necessary reference, to *Measure for Measure;* and the product of the borrowings is hardly a translation or a pastiche but a poetic production on the same theme as the sources but in very altered form. This last point is perhaps the most interesting aspect of Tennyson studies. In the case of *Mariana,* Tennyson borrowed from an epic, a drama, and a lyric. The result cannot be said to be any one of these: indeed, part of the fascination of *Mariana* is its playful distinction of form. Somewhat like a ballad, it is not a ballad; somewhat lyrical, it is too detached in its narrative to be truly a lyric. We can recognize *Mariana* for what it really is, of course, from Tennyson's later work. It is an idyll. But this most vexing of Tennysonian terms will require a separate chapter of explanation.

TWO

The Sources of Tennyson's Idyll

AFTER THE PUBLICATION of Browning's *Dramatic Idylls* in 1879, Tennyson complained to William Allingham, "I wish Browning had not taken my word Idyll."[1] Indeed, by 1879 Tennyson was entitled to feel he had a proprietary right to the term, for both the English Idyls and *The Idylls of the King* were behind him, and his work had largely defined whatever meaning idyll has in the English tradition.

But what exactly did Tennyson mean by idyll? That he had a clear and detailed notion of its meaning is clear from his distinction between idyl and idyll. (Throughout this book the form idyll is used for the sake of convenience except where Tennyson's title English Idyls is mentioned.) Hallam Tennyson explains the distinction between the two forms as one of length: "My father used to spell Idyls with one 'l' for the shorter Idyls, and Idylls with two 'l's for the epic Idylls of the King,"[2] but Tennyson himself is silent on the purpose of two terms, and a domestic idyl like *Enoch Arden* is longer than anything in *The Idylls of the King*. Thus it is not at first easy to understand what Tennyson's idea of idyll incorporated.

The use of the term idyll in antiquity is surrounded by similar ambiguity, and the lack of clarity in the classical tradition in part explains Tennyson's own apparent vagueness on the subject. This vagueness is only apparent, however, for Tennyson seems to have imposed a formal order on the classical confusion and worked out his own conception of the generic heritage. But in fact Theocritus and the other Alexandrian poets who wrote what Tennyson and the modern world would consider idylls did not use the expression. As late as Pliny's time the term was still a muddle, as Pliny's comment in one of his letters presenting his friend Paternus with a volume of his poems illustrates: "Proinde, sive epigrammata sive idyllia sive eclogas sive, ut multi, poematia seu quod aliud vocare malueris, licebit voces" (4:14) ("Call these poems epigrams, or idylls, or eclogues, or as many others have, little poems—call them what you like"). For Pliny as for Tennyson, the word idyll seemed capable of being applied to the whole range of short poetry on the Alexandrian models.

In English there is no consensus about the term either; it is infrequently used in the titles of English poems before Tennyson, whose clearest indebtedness for this form is to Walter Savage Landor. Landor's early poetry evidences the same fascination with the Alexandrian traditions that Tennyson's does, and works like his *Fiesolan Idyl* of 1831 show him quite consciously working in the tradition that Tennyson would later exploit to the fullest. But Landor's most characteristic and influential experiments in Alexandrian forms came after, not before, Tennyson had embarked on his own variations on idyll: Landor's *Hellenics* was published in 1846 and his *Heroic Idyls* a year before his death in 1863. Thus there was no clear English tradition of idyll on which Tennyson could draw, and even his use of the term seems to add little clarity: the disparate forms of the English Idyls and *The Idylls of the King* hardly fit comfortably under a single rubric, even one with a dual spelling.

And yet idyll is a term central to Tennyson's poetry, and the attempt should be made to understand what he meant by it. Perhaps it was the very ambiguity of the form that attracted him, for the confusion provided almost boundless leeway for the craftsman to define and shape the tradition in his own way: thus, the idyll was perfectly suited to Tennyson's craving to treat the poetic tradition as a plastic source to be used, not imitated. Clearly, his use of the term idyll, like Wordworth's and Coleridge's use of "lyrical ballad," implies a carefully considered and original definition by which he related a new poetic effusion to an older tradition in an esemplastic way, to use Coleridge's term for the process; and like Wordsworth's and Coleridge's conception of lyrical ballad, Tennyson's idea of idyll did not readily correspond to any rigorous or historical definition of the genre. This is not surprising, for Tennyson's view of the tradition was broad and inclusive, and he had little time for neat, scholarly precision in the delineation of forms. After compiling *The Golden Treasury* Francis Palgrave once had doubts about including sonnets and elegies among the *Treasury*'s "English Lyrical Poems," because he felt, "the Greeks classified elegies as non-lyrical, and they had no sonnets."[3] Tennyson had been the final arbiter in the choice of poems for the *Treasury*, and his response to this narrow formalism can be inferred from the catholic selection of forms that compose the anthology.

A similar catholicity was brought to bear by Tennyson in the definition of idyll, which in his work designates poems that might more strictly be classified as dramatic monologue, dialogue, epyllion, elegy, satire, or lyric. It is, then, among these classical forms and their English adaptations—the stock of poety through which the exact definition of the term idyll has traditionally been debated—that we must look for Tennyson's models and for the connections between them that would have justified him in believing that they made up a common tradition. For more than one hundred years, critics have categorized Tennyson's poetry as Alexandrian and noted the similarities between his verse and the forms of poetry loosely classified as idyll that evolved in the Hellenistic period.[4] These comparisons contain much truth, but they cannot be fully appreciated without an exact knowledge of what the Alexandrian forms of poetry were and why Tennyson felt they could be understood under the single term idyll. For the sake of this argument, the term idyll will be used in the same inclusive way in which Tennyson employed it and will cover the range of poetry on which he most heavily relied in the formation of his verse, though this approach to idyll reflects Tennyson's use of the term rather than modern scholarship.

The word idyll, from the Greek *eidyllion*, is, even in its

possible roots, a controversial term. It may mean "little picture," as is often claimed, or it may reflect an interest in poetic structure, since the word from which it derives, *eidos*, meaning shape, form, figure, and hence species, nicely captures the Alexandrian preoccupation with genre and poetic form. Although the poets who first wrote what Tennyson would have called idylls did not use this term to describe their own work, others applied it to their poetry, and, later in antiquity, to any short poetic form. The confusion inherent in the term idyll is only compounded by turning to Hellenistic poetry, particularly that of Theocritus, Callimachus, Bion, and Moschus, from which Tennyson drew so much, and seeking to define idyll in terms of subject matter, meter, length, or any other property. All these elements, even length, varied widely in Hellenistic poetry. Some idylls were well under 100 lines, while the *Aetia* of Callimachus, a collection of separate but related poems that are usually in forms Tennyson would have called idyllic, probably ran to some 4,000 lines altogether.

The basic difficulty in confronting the idyll form stems from two attributes it shares with much other poetry but stresses as no other body of verse does: self-consciousness and eclecticism. All poetry may be by definition self-conscious, but in the poetry of the Alexandrians, which later came to be called idyll, self-consciousness was raised to the level of a ruling conceit: the originators of idyll were fully aware that they were creating a new form and went about their business with a scholarly zeal for precision and detail, twin academic passions that produced in their poetry an unparalleled effect of conscious distance and manipulation of form. The idyll may be the first poetic structure that can be said to have been researched into existence. The earliest practitioners of the form were learned men who held "academic" positions in their society; the most quoted of the Alexandrians in antiquity, Callimachus, was chief librarian of the famous collection in the Museum at Alexandria. In this capacity he produced a catalogue of the Museum's books, the *Pinakes*, which listed every volume in the vast collection. Theocritus too was associated with the learned world of Ptolemaic Alexandria, as was Apollonius of

Rhodes, the pupil of Callimachus who feuded with his master over the proper form of poetry. The learning of the founders of the idyll form is manifested in their poetry in two main modes of self-consciousness, erudition and distance. A patina of erudition is a distinctive feature of many idylls, especially those of Callimachus and his disciples. This feature is most apparent in the elaborate paraphrases of lines such as

καὶ πρόκατε γνωτὸς Μέμνονος Αἰθίοπος
ἵετο κυκλώσας βαλιὰ πτερὰ θῆλυς ἀήτης,
ἵππος ἰοζώνου Λοκρίδος Ἀρσινόης, (*Aetia* 110.52–54)

in which Callimachus, meaning only that the west wind, Zephyr, moved his wings, says with great elaboration, "And forthwith the gentle breeze, the brother of Ethiopian Memnon and the steed of violet-girdled Locrian Arsinoë, moved in circles his swift wings."[5] The extensive scholarship of the idyll's creators found its way not only into the often elaborate rhetoric of the idyll form, but also into its stories, which drew on obscure and recondite aspects of mythology as well as life.

The second and perhaps more characteristic trait of the idyll, which can in part be attributed to its learned originators, is its distance from the reader. Distance is achieved in several ways, the most common being the framing device, frequently employed in Theocritus' pastoral pieces, in which the central poem, perhaps a love song or a dirge, is set off by conversation between two shepherds who challenge each other to a singing contest. The framing device, which reminds the reader of the artificiality of the situation, vitiates any emotional immediacy that might be conveyed by the central poetic material. But even as emotional involvement is curbed by the distance created by the poet, aesthetic reflection is encouraged, and the reader is invited to see the poetry from a vantage point beyond feeling—a vantage point purged of ephemeral emotionality that will allow him to discern the true shape or form of the poem and its subject. (Hence, perhaps, the name *eidyllion*, stressing this aspect of form.) Although the idyll discusses passion frequently, it almost invariably does so in a distant and passionless way, suggesting Keats's term "cold pastoral." This purposeful dissociation of emotion from art points to the handiwork of the scholar rather than the afflatus of the poet. The framing device, coupled with the allusive nature of the poetry and its often idealized or decorated situations, compels the work to be studied as artifact instead of as inspiration.[6]

Besides being self-conscious, the idyll form is also eclectic in that it borrows, in pack-rat fashion, from the whole of the literature that precedes it. The use of tradition is of course common in some degree to all poetry, but in the Alexandrians it is a central preoccupation infusing all their work. Alexandrian poetry forces the reader to become conscious of the tradition used, whereas in much other poetry it is the business of the craftsman to avoid awakening an awareness of tradition. Once again, part of the impetus for this use of tradition lies in the scholarly nature of the idyll's creators. The Alexandrians had before them for study the entire cultural product of the ancient world down to their time, and in the process of cataloguing and editing this bulk, they must have suffered what was probably the first case of anxiety over literary influence. Latent in the Hellenistic idylls is the recognition that the great things have already been done and that poetry must now imitate scholarship by collecting and analyzing poetic traditions. Indeed, the idyll form is in many respects an amalgam of the primary forms of Greek literature prior to the Hellenistic period.

This is not to say that the idyll is a réchauffé of the early Greek forms. It is, in its recombination of earlier materials, an entirely new genre, but its originality lies not in its departure from the established norms but in its manipulation of them. The idyll is culturally omnivorous, and its plays with its sources; in fact, the reader can feel, even if he is ignorant of it, the playfulness in the poetry, with the result that he may dismiss the idyll as trivial or lightweight.

To turn to the generic origins of the idyll, Homer was of course foremost in the minds of the Hellenistic writers. Callimachus' debate with his pupil Apollonius centered on the question of whether it was profitable to imitate the Homeric epic; Callimachus felt that since Homer could not be improved upon, he should not be copied. (This was not an objection to *long* forms, as Callimachus' position is often intepreted; it was rather an objection to *old* forms; Callimachus could hardly have objected to length when his foremost poem was of epic proportions.)[7] But while the Hellenistic poets generally followed Callimachus in eschewing the Homeric epic form, they borrowed much else from Homer. First, they adapted the Homeric mythology, using it as a point of departure for developing a new theory of myth, yet one that was rooted in the traditional Homeric texts taught to every Greek child. A good example of the process is Theocritus' *Cyclops* (Idyll XI), in which Polyphemus is made to sing a love song to the sea nymph Galatea. Homer's Cyclops was a monster who epitomized everything the Greek world considered uncivilized; Theocritus' Cyclops is the pathetic victim of an unrequited love. The Cyclops is the same figure in both poems, but the myth was used to vastly different effect by Theocritus, who was interested in psychic and emotional phenomena of which Homer's society had possibly been oblivious. Theocritus purposely chose the Cyclops because of his repulsive reputation in the Homeric canon; he could then demonstrate that even the most debased creature was part of the amatory nexus that constituted the Theocritean universe, and by selecting the most debased creature, he could examine what was fundamental in that nexus, for Polyphemus represented the lowest common denominator of feeling. Idyll XI is set off, in typical idyll fashion, with a framing device, and throughout the poem, which is one of the loveliest of the Alexandrian school, runs the cool, almost clinical detachment that marks the form. The Homeric myth of the Cyclops, which is detached from the plot that surrounded it in Homer, is treated in such a way that Polyphemus ceases to be a real figure, as he is in the *Odyssey*, and becomes in part an allegorical representation of the mind working under the influence of an overmastering passion.

By thus appropriating the machinery of the Homeric epic for the study of psychological states, the idyll developed the foundations for the Western tradition of allegory. Alexandria was traditionally a center for allegory. Philo produced his allegorical reconciliation of the Septuagint and Platonic philosophy there, and the Alexandrian church relied on allegory as a textual method. This allegorical interest seems to have been indigenous to the city, for the idylls of Theocritus and his school also savor of it. With Vergil's use of the idyll, as Servius pointed out, allegory was fully developed in this poetic form. Allegory, of course, is another distancing literary device, compelling the reader to see that the immediate text is only a reference to a higher truth, not directly apprehended. The effect of this allegorical bent is also evident in the idylls of later writers, especially Tennyson.

Besides Homer's mythology, which it borrowed and turned to its own purposes, the idyll took from the epic its meter and (more difficult to define) its pretensions. Between the Homeric and the Hellenistic ages the hexameter of the epic suffered a certain desuetude. The Alexandrian poets, who under the leadership of Callimachus professed the desire to avoid the format of the Homeric epic, nonetheless revived its meter, and in so doing they indicated that the idyll, while it would be different from the epic, would at least be epic in intent. The idyll is by design grander than the lyric, which at first glance would seem to have offered the natural meters for the shorter, more confined, and emotionally descriptive structure of the idyll. Built into the idyll, and consciously so, is an epic aspiration to reach universal and sweeping conclusions, though in a different area from the epic, and the natural verse form to accomplish this is the hexameter of the *Iliad* and the *Odyssey*. Of course, idyllic verse need not be written in hexameters; Callimachus' idyllic *Aetia* is not, while his *Hecale* is; in Theocritus, however, the hexameter predominates, and with the Roman descendants of the Alexandrians the idyll often uses the hexameter of epic universality.

Just as Polyphemus was differently interpreted by Theocritus and by Homer, so too the concept of "universality" was altered by the idyllic poets. In the Homeric epic, universality, or the appearance of it, is achieved through a large narrative embracing a wide variety of characters and personalities who are engaged in a central action that is sufficiently significant not only to affect each member of society but also to evoke the intervention of the deities. This concept of epic sweep is almost diametrically opposed to that professed in the idyll form, for the idyll concentrates, as Callimachus had wanted it to, on events that, like the Cyclops' plaint to Galatea, are isolated from any larger context. The number of characters in the idyll is severely limited (usually there are no more than two speaking characters), and the action, if there is any, affects only the isolated protagonist of the idyll itself, as in Theocritus' *The Spell* (Idyll II), in which a woman, thinking herself betrayed in love, invokes the curse of Hecate on her faithless lover. In this poem, the Homeric epic deities have not been eliminated, but rather have been replaced by gods and goddesses of a different order—Hecate, Eros, and Aphrodite, whose Homeric role had been slight. Whereas Zeus and the Olympians presided over an epic order that was grand, socially embodied, and palpably real, the gods of the idyll rule over certain intangible emotive or mental states (jealousy, anger, desire), and these gods provide the clue to an understanding of the epic pretension of the idyll form: it seeks universality in a comprehensive survey of the continuum of human feeling.[8] Hence the fragmentation and lack of narrative connections in the idyll: human feelings do not fit neatly together in the shape of a plot; fragmentation describes the human condition.

But it would be wrong to argue from this lack of narrative unity that the idyll has no cohesion.[9] The connections between different idylls are often subtle and hidden, like the links between various psychological states, but they are there. With the Greeks these links may not be easily discovered because of the state of the texts that have survived. It is possible, however, to infer from a study of Vergil and Ovid, whose poems are often linked by a thread of themes and echoes, that their Hellenistic models also possessed a sort of narrative of mental states, or a unity of feeling, and in the case of Theocritus this unity can be demonstrated.[10] Whereas the epic had sought to depict unity in the human community and the forces governing it, the idyll turned to the heart to search for its generalities. The two approaches overlapped each other, but they required different forms in which to express their discoveries.

From the epic, then, the idyll borrowed the fundamentals

of its mythology, the epic meter, and the epic claim to universality; but in each case the idyll altered these concepts to fit an altered conception of life. An analogous process occurred when the idyll borrowed from the Greek melic poetry of Mimnermus, Archilochus, Sappho, and Alcaeus. As with the epic, the idyll took from the lyric what suited its needs, altering what it borrowed in the process. The lyric was, in the Greek world, a sung form, and the convention that the characters of the idyll often sing is a direct importation from the lyric form. The idyll, however, was probably not sung, which would be a natural development for a form given to reflection. So in Theocritus' Idyll I, when Thyrsis sings the lament for Daphnis, he evokes not the lyric, but the memory of the lyric. The idyll form makes the reader conscious that the forms it draws on are not being used in their original functions, and this device emphasizes its artificiality.

In the same way that it adapted the convention of singing, the idyll took from the lyric the use of the first person. But, once again, whereas in the lyric the speaker (in the first person singular) has traditionally been identified with the poet, in the idyll the first person usage is a literary convention that in all probability has nothing to do with the author. Sappho had written,

ἀ δέ μ' ἴδρως κακχέεται, τρόμος δὲ
παῖσαν ἄγρει, χλωροτέρα δὲ ποίας
ἔμμι, τεθνάκην δ' ὀλίγω 'πιδεύης
φαίνομ' ἔμ' αὔτᾳ. (Frag. 2)

Sweat pours down me; trembling seizes every limb. Greener than grass am I, and I seem to be little short of dying.

Whether she is speaking of herself in these lines (as critics have usually assumed), or not, the reader—or originally, the listener—is presented with an immediate statement of someone in love. The lover's interior feelings are portrayed without an intermediate commentary or device, and this is the central conceit of all lyric: that the reader is directly experiencing the interior life of some other individual like himself or herself. But when Theocritus and the makers of idyll took over the lyric tradition, which was some four hundred years old when they inherited it, they affected a slight change that fundamentally altered the lyric premise. In Theocritus' rendition of these Sapphic lines,

$$\text{ἐκ δὲ μετώπω}$$
$$\text{ἰδρώς μευ κοχύδεσκεν ἴσον νοτίαισιν ἐέρσαις} \quad (2.106–107)$$

From my forehead sweat gushed out like wet dews,

the immediacy of Sappho's lyric is gone, though the shell of words remains. In this idyll the speaker is explicitly a jealous woman involved in sorcery, and the reader is invited, not to participate in her emotions, as in the lyric, but to reflect upon them. The lyric elements in idyll are used as a source of contemplation, not involvement, and this tendency in idyll may partially explain its pastoral convention: the countryside in which the idyll is often set is a deliberately distant environment (especially to the city-dwelling audience of the original Alexandrian idylls) that is meant to further vitiate any lyric immediacy.

Since the idyll purposely makes its speakers distinct from the author's sensibilities, it would be natural for the form to have affinities with the drama, and this is indeed the case. The idyll often creates a dramatic situation, with two speaking characters, or one speaking and one dumb character, as in Theocritus' *Spell*, in which a female slave is spoken to but never speaks. This dramatic convention has been traced to the idyll's development from the much older mime form, particularly the mimes of Sophron and the comedies of Epicharmus, who wrote in the sixth and fifth centuries and whose works were a source of comfort and amusement to Plato. Although very little of the works of Sophron or Epicharmus remains, we know that they consisted of a contest, or agon, between two characters and were couched in an earthy and amusing style. The many idylls that use the agon format (Theocritus' Idylls IV, V, VI, VII) attest to the form's borrowing from the mime. The idyll may also have borrowed its numerous shepherds and frequent Sicilian locales from Sophron's work.

But if the writers of idylls took over from Sophron the amusing banter of Sicilian shepherds, their inherent desire to isolate and study mental states often dictated that the agon, or speaking contest of the mime, give way to monologue, and here the idyll blended mime, the ludicrous rustic genre, with Athenian drama, the loftiest expression of dramatic form known to the Greeks. Theocritus' *Spell* may preserve the mime format, but the intensity of the jealous lover's passions are closer to the emotions expressed in the monologues of Euripides, say in his *Medea*. The Alexandrians shared with Euripides and the Aristotelian school of philosophers a deep interest in psychological typology (Theophrastus was in this regard a natural forerunner of the idyllic poets), and many idylls tend to downplay the role of the second speaker from the mime and present a dramatic monologue,[11] as in the pseudo-Theocritean *Rustic* (Idyll XX), in which the speaker is certainly not the lyric "I"; he is presented instead as a study of the human personality reacting under emotional stimulus:

> Εὐνίκα μ' ἐγέλαξε θελοντά ἁδὺ φιλᾶσαι
> καί μ' ἐπικερτομέοισα τάδ' ἔννεπεν· "ἔρρ' ἀπ' ἐμεῖο.
> βουκόλος ὢν ἐθέλεις με κύσαι, τάλαν; οὐ μεμάθηκα
> ἀγροίκως φιλέειν, ἀλλ' ἀστικὰ χείλεα θλίβειν.
> μὴ τύγε μευ κύσσῃς τὸ καλὸν στόμα μηδ' ἐν ὀνείροις.
>
> . . . . .
>
> τοιάδε μυθίζοισα τρὶς εἰς ἑὸν ἔπτυσε κόλπον,
> καί μ' ἀπὸ τᾶς κεφαλᾶς ποτὶ τὼ πόδε συνεχὲς εἶδεν
> χείλεσι μυχθίζοισα καὶ ὄμμασι λοξὰ βλέποισα,
> καὶ πολὺ τᾷ μορφᾷ θηλύνετο, καί τι σεσαρός
> καὶ σοβαρόν μ' ἐγέλαξεν. ἐμοὶ δ' ἄφαρ ἔζεσεν αἷμα,
> καὶ χρόα φοινίχθην ὑπὸ τὤλγεος ῥόδον ἔρσᾳ.
> χᾷ μὲν ἔβα με λιποῖσα, φέρω δ' ὑποκάρδιον ὀργάν,
> ὅττι με τὸν χαρίεντα κακὰ μωμήσαθ' ἑταίρα.   (1–5, 11–18)

Eunica mocked me when I would have sweetly kissed her, and, taunting me, thus said: "Begone from me. Wouldst thou kiss me, wretch, thou that art a neatherd? I have not learnt to kiss rustics but to press gentle lips; and as for thee, kiss not my fair lips even in thy dreams . . ." With such words as these she spat thrice into her bosom, and eyed me over from head to foot with angry glance and mouth of disgust, and with many a ladylike air, open-mouthed and insolent she mocked me. Straight my blood boiled, and at the smart I crimsoned as a rose with dew. And she went off and left me; but deep

in my heart I nurse my wrath that this vile light of love
should slight the pretty fellow that I am.

The bumpkin speaking might be a study from Theophrastus'
Characters, but he is presented with the wit of the mime
and his song incorporates the sweetness of the lyric. He
delivers a monologue such as might be heard on stage, but
this portrait of him contributes to the Alexandrians' epic
compendium of the human psyche.

The idyll, like the mime, is an earthy, even a realistic
form. This is a curious assertion to make about a form that
is so acutely stylized and self-consciously artificial. And
yet it is true; Theocritus' shepherds may sing in Doric
hexameters, but they are quite capable of incorporating in
those hexameters the language of the Sicilian meadows:

> ἁνίκ' ἐπύγιζόν τυ, τὺ δ' ἄλγεες· αἱ δὲ χίμαιραι
> αἵδε κατεβληχῶντο, καὶ ὁ τράγος αὐτὰς ἐτρύπη. (V, 41–42)

While I was buggering you and you called out in pain, the
nanny-goats bleated in derision and the goat screwed them.

Because Hellenistic idyll often employs dialect—the Greek
of these idylls is definitely not like Pope's English—its language is sometimes styled hyper-Doric, after the Doric dialect of Sicily, the locale of many of the pastoral idylls. The
term is a useful one, for it indicates that the poet makes the
speakers of the idylls use false Doric forms fashioned by
analogy with genuine ones, thereby overindulging colloquial
realism until it becomes artificial.[12] In effect, the idyll form
as a whole is artificial not because it is less than realistic, but
because it is more than realistic. This extreme realism is in
part attributable to the form's origins in mime.

But the mime was not merely a source of local color and
dramatic amusement for the idyll, though it was both of
these. Plato and the Hellenistic world found the comedic
drama form that antedated the idyll instructive, and the
statue of Epicharmus at Syracuse bore an inscription honor-
ing him because "he told the children many things that are
useful in life,"

> πολλὰ γὰρ ποττὰν ζόαν ταῖς παισὶν εἶπε χρήσιμα.
> (Theocritean inscription 18.9)

Chresima does not bear a moral interpretation, and the idyll, following the mime, is not didactic; it is meant to impart useful information. The idyll, like the mime, is "useful" because it demonstrates the range of human feeling; one is not told what to think in the idyll form, but only shown, from a proper distance, what the shape of the psyche is. It was perhaps this aspect of the comedies of Epicharmus that Plato enjoyed, and it was certainly this aspect of the mime that was incorporated into the Hellenistic idyll. Because Plato used the mime form as one source for the structure of his dialogues, the idyll not only borrowed from the mime, but from Plato's adaptation of it: the *Phaedrus* must constantly have been in the mind of Theocritus as he explored the erotic filaments that bound his universe; and the humorous detachment that belies an absolute seriousness —the Socratic trademark—is also the posture of all idylls. Even the artistic detachment of the idyll is Platonic, in that the idyll consciously draws the reader's attention to its formal properties, from which the reader is dissociated. This is analogous to the Platonic method of drawing the student's attention away from the created world and directing it toward the contemplation of the disembodied forms that constitute the real universe. Idyll likewise draws attention to form and seeks knowledge of the disembodied states. The idyll, in fact, may be considered the Platonic mode of poetry.

The idyll also has roots in drama outside the mime. It is wrong, for instance, to conceive of idyll as only a pretty form derived from mime and written by citified Alexandrians, but dealing with an enameled and false countryside. This view is far too one-sided. As befitted a genre that developed while Euripides was the most popular playwright in revival and while New Comedy was in its ascendancy, the idyll was versatile enough to deal with emotional situations in terms that seemed relevant and contemporary to a third-century Alexandrian. Theocritus' *Adonis Festival* (Idyll XV) is perhaps the best example of this. In this idyll two middle-class matrons of Alexandria prattle on about the trials of maintaining a household and the difficulties of navigating the streets during this, the chief religious holiday of the city. The poem perserves the mime form; it is contemporary and realistic in its locale; it incorporates a dirge for Adonis in stark contrast to the domestic chatter of its central characters; and it is written in the Homeric meter. In short, it shows the idyll at its baffling and eclectic heights, and it dispels the notion that idyll and pastoral are necessarily the same. A pastoral may need to be an idyll, but an idyll is definitely not of necessity a pastoral.

The idyll, then, is a form compounded of contradictions. It is aloof, the work of meticulous scholars consciously manipulating the genre; yet its subject matter is the human psyche and its speakers sing with lyric immediacy. It is a form that, at least with Callimachus, declares a type of war on the epic, and yet it strives for epic fullness and frequently employs the Homeric meter. It is a decidedly pretty form that often hearkens to the beauties of the shepherd world, and yet it moves as easily in the same realms of contemporary social comedy as the New Comedy of Menander. It is artificial; yet it employs an extreme form of realism. It depicts song and revels in artistry; yet is "useful to life." Small wonder, then, that so protean a form can be taken as a variety of genres: Theocritus' *Thyrsis*, containing the lament for Daphnis, is an elegy in the modern sense; Callimachus' *Hecale* is an epyllion, a short elaboration of tradition mythology; and the Sicilian pieces of Theocritus are pastorals. But this subdivision of the idyll overlooks the factors common to all these poems—broadly, self-consciousness and eclecticism, qualities that are found in abundance in the poetry of Tennyson and that in his mind united the tradition.

This often paradoxical, self-reflective, and allusive body of verse the Hellenistic world bequeathed to the Roman poets, who both preserved and developed it. Not that the Romans either wanted or were able to adopt the idyll without altering it. For one thing, the Greek meters, especially the hexameter, resisted easy imitation in Latin, and this difficulty was not finally overcome until Vergil perfected the epic meter in his native language. (Tennyson preferred the meters of the Lesbian poets Sappho and Alcaeus to the imitations of them in Horace's *Odes*, almost certainly because the Horatian imitations are stiff and uneasy by comparison with their originals; his preference illuminates one of the difficulties the Romans faced in translating the Alexandrian innovations into their own tongue.)[13] Perhaps because of technical problems of this nature, and also because of a *gravitas* in the Roman character that precluded exact imitation of their more playful models, the Latin idyll tends to be, like the hexameters in which it is often written, a more decorous and rigid creation than the poetry of Alexandria. But the willingness of the Latin poets to confront the technical problems of the idyll indicates their desire to incorporate the form into Latin at any cost.

The poetry of Catullus reveals the same desire to mix and experiment with forms that marked the Hellenistic school, as well as the longing for formal unity and epic theme. This longing found its way into his epyllia (LXVI, for instance), and into the structure of his poetry, for the Roman poets arranged their verse, as Theocritus had his, so that motifs and themes would connect their short works as plot and narrative had unified the poetry of the Heroic Age. Even in Latin elegiac poetry, where the idyll is not an immediately apparent influence, the Alexandrian form had done its work: in Propertius the traditional "I" is no longer the real poet, but the persona of the idyll; his elegies are an elaborate artistic fabrication, not the immediate cries of a man in love, and Cynthia, though she may have existed in life, is treated almost as mythically as the Cyclops.[14]

The most devoted Latin disciples of the Hellenistic school were also Rome's two greatest poets—Vergil and Ovid. Each one took the idyll form, perfected it through imitation, and then pressed it beyond its original bounds. While Vergil's experiments with the Hellenistic forms were both earlier and more stunning than Ovid's, Ovid's provide a neater textbook example of the way in which the Roman poets expropriated the form.

Ovid's greatest and most influential work, the *Metamorphoses*, is essentially a series of idylls extended to epic length. This was in itself not a formal innovation, for Callimachus' *Aetia* had followed much the same plan. But while little of the *Aetia* remains, all of the *Metamorphoses* has come down to us, and we can see in it what we could only guess at in Callimachus, that it has *unity*.[15] This is a very striking achievement, for the subject of the *Metamorphoses*, as its title suggests, is change and transformation, and its materials are the disparate myths of the Greco-Roman world, which Ovid treats in a series of epyllia. To have brought formal stability to these materials and themes was an accomplishment of considerable formal skill, for it finally reconciled the innovative, psychological yearnings of the idyll, usually expressed in short and fragmentary studies of individuals, with the form's epic pretensions. This Ovid accomplished by weaving a "perpetuum carmen," a continuum of poetry from the earliest times to his own (*Met.* 1.3–4).[16] Myth and history weave in and out of the Ovidian scheme until they become indistinguishable: the historical explanation of the world is mythic, but perhaps more important, the mythic history of changes as presented in the *Metamorphoses* acquires an historical validity that gives the poem the same kind of formal unity as, say, Livy's *History*. Ovid consistently worked within the idyllic tradition, and his *Fasti*, which organizes epyllia around the Roman calendar, betrays the same longing to bring structural unity to the idyll when the form is extended in length.

But Vergil had gone beyond these frontiers even before Ovid. Everything that Vergil wrote, from the *Eclogues* through the *Aeneid*, may be said to have been influenced by the idyll form, but as true as this is, it does little justice to the amazing skill with which he strengthened and transformed the forms in which he worked. Vergil's earliest poems, as far as we know them, are close imitations of the Alexandrian models, and this imitation takes its highest expression in his *Eclogues*, ten connected poems in which the pastoral idyll is perfected. Here all the tendencies of the idyll stand in clear relief. The mime form is preserved; the poems are eclectic (this time the source is the Alexandrians themselves); they exist at a distance, but their subject is the human heart; and the epic proportion is present, not only in the fourth, messianic eclogue, where Vergil exclaims, "paulo maiore canamus" ("let us sing a larger song"), but in the structure of the whole work. Love is the theme throughout—love defined as the passion of the human heart and mind for unity and peace—and the *Eclogues* investigate this theme from ten different points of view, gracefully shifting between attitudes with a kind of Lockean association of ideas. As in any form that attempts to demonstrate psychological states through speaking characters, as the idyll in general and the *Eclogues* in particular do, there is also a strong tendency to allegory. Vergil's foremost critic, Servius, writing in the late fourth or early early fifth century, annotated the *Eclogues* so that the connection between allegory and idyll, which had been present earlier in the work of Theocritus, would never again be forgotten.[17]

The *Georgics* continue the use of idyll (the fourth *Georgic*, for instance, contains an epyllion), but Vergil's great innovation in the use of the idyll came when he applied the lessons he had learned from his study of Hellenistic poetry to restructuring the epic. His aim was essentially that of the Greek fashioners of the idyll: to create a form that would respect the tradition and yet be responsive to the world in which he lived. That world, unlike Homer's, possessed a sense of history something like our own and a fascination with the individual's interior structure. Vergil's use of elements of the idyll to alter the Homeric epic form he had inherited is most obviously illustrated by Book IV of the *Aeneid*, the romance of Dido and Aeneas. In this book, which is fundamentally an epyllion, Vergil gives a mythic-historic explanation of the enmity between Rome and Carthage (in this regard the book is an *aetion* in the manner of Callimachus, an examination of the cause of something) while at the same time presenting a psychological portrait of a character, Dido, in the fashion of Theocritus' *Cyclops* idyll. (Even the mime's two-character format is preserved in the interplay of Dido and her sister Anna.) This mixture of *aetion* and dramatic idyll with traditional epic had repercussions for the whole epic tradition, which may be observed in Vergil's Italian descendants, Dante and Tasso. The *Commedia*, with its succession of allegorical-cum-historical character portraits in Hell, Purgatory, and Heaven, is a variation on the epic which was only possible under the influence of the idyll, and the introduction of romance into the epic structure in Tasso and Ariosto, far from being a revolution in genre, was a simple progression from Vergil's fourth book, written under the Alexandrian influence.

In one final way the Alexandrian idyll influenced Latin poetry. The Romans were painfully conscious of their indebtedness to the Hellenistic poets in most things, but the form of satire they considered indigenous to Italy: "tota nostra est," Quintilian said of it (10.1.93). But the claim seems not to have been true, for satire as exhibited in Horace and in Juvenal shows definite affinities with the mime and with the idyll in its manifestation as monologue.[18] Several of Horace's *Satires* are mimes (for example, 1.9, 2.1, 2.3, 2.4), and one is an outright monologue (2.2). Juvenal's satires take with one exception the monologue form, and his third satire evidences his indebtedness to the Alexandrian tradition: the poem is in the form of a monologue, placed in the mouth of his friend Umbricius as he leaves Rome for the countryside, and the contrast between the unnatural city and the pastoral world toward which Umbricius is headed is an essential feature of Juvenal's denunciation of Roman society. Of course, these Latin adaptations of the monologue go a long way beyond the form as seen in Theocritus' *Rustic*. They envelop more of the social milieu, they are sharper in attack, and they are what idyll never is, judgmental. This last aspect, demonstrated particularly in Horace, may in fact be the genuine Roman contribution to the idyll form. The moral or ethical dimension, added to the dramatic monologue form of the idyll by the Romans, is now an essential part of the definition of satire, though in the dramatic monologues of the nineteenth century it is more likely to crop up in the work of Browning than of Tennyson.

From the Latin tradition, the idyll, as modified by the Roman poets, descended to English poetry of the Renaissance. Donne's amatory epistles, for instance, are a reworking of the idyll as dramatic monologue,[19] written in direct imitation of Ovid's *Amores*. Marvell's *To His Coy Mistress* and his *Nymph Complaining for the Death of Her Fawn* are in the same tradition, while his Mower poems are closer to the Theocritean originals than to Ovid in their poignant delicacy; his pastoral dialogues (for example, *Thyrsis and Dorinda* and *Clorinda and Damon*) are direct imitations of the Alexandrian mime-idyll. And Milton, like Vergil, used the idyll as the groundwork for a whole poetic career. *L' Allegro* and *Il Penseroso* are, like their Theocritean models, idyllic examinations of fixed emotional states, but in them Milton formalized the tendency of idyll toward allegory.

Lycidas and the early elegies are experiments in the genre established by Theocritus, Bion, and Moschus, with the important difference that in *Lycidas* Milton adapted the lore of Christendom to serve the function that Homeric myth had served for the Alexandrians: it provided him with a commonly held body of reference that he could expand and embroider in new and surprising ways. *On the Morning of Christ's Nativity* is an earlier Miltonic example of the Hellenistic sensibility at work; in that poem Milton treats the birth of Christ as the idyllic poets were fond of treating the myths surrounding Hercules: he takes the received tradition and builds a new mythic layer on top of it, a process akin to that followed by Theocritus in his *Cyclops*.

Paradise Lost, of course, is the culmination of Milton's studies in the idyll, much as the *Aeneid* was for Vergil. As anthologizers have long since discovered, Books IV and IX of Milton's epic, along with Books I and II taken together, can stand alone, on the model of epyllia. (Homer, on the other hand, is very difficult to anthologize; his work is a narrative whole.) Each book is an extended reworking of received materials in the heightened style of the idyll, and Book IV is a conscious adaptation of the pastoral idyll to the purposes of a Christian epic. The potential of the idyll to make general observations about the human psyche was naturally attractive to Milton in his epic ambitions, for his plan was an overall picture of the state of the soul: the difference between Theocritius' Rustic and Milton's Adam and Eve is that the former is descriptive of only one psychic state while in the latter pair Milton attempted to incorporate the entire range of human psychology. As with Callimachus, Vergil, and Ovid, the interwoven idylls that make up *Paradise Lost* are given not only as myth but as historical fact, and the two are woven together in such a way as to suggest that there is no valid distinction between them; in Milton the claim that is latent in Callimachus' *Aetia* is perfected— the poet is the final historian of the nature and causes of the universe.

In the eighteenth century the idyll was not used on a scale comparable with Milton's. Instead the various manifestations of the form were classified and polished in their original, classical shapes. Gray's *Elegy* is perhaps the most perfect expression in any language of the idyll as threnody. Gray and Pope refined the pastoral idyll, and even the supposedly mock pastoral, in which the eighteenth-century city was treated as the pastoral milieu, had its roots in the idyll tradition of Theocritus, who had used Alexandria in much the same way in his *Adonis Festival*. The dramatic-monologue form of the idyll was extensively employed in the eighteenth century; Pope's *Eloisa to Abelard* and *The Dying Christian* are early examples of the type; Cowper's *Alexander Selkirk* is a late use. What the eighteenth century primarily brought to the idyll was not massive vision, as Milton had done, but social sensibility: Gray's *Elegy*, for instance, is not a lament for a single individual, or even a single individual as allegorically representative of some human condition; it is an elegy for a whole class. Even the dramatic-monologue form of the idyll, since its protagonists in the eighteenth century tended to be people in isolation, like Eloisa or Selkirk, was used as a vehicle for examining social consciousness through a study of the effects of the deprivation of human companionship upon the individual. The idyll had always been psychological in the broadest sense of the term. In the eighteenth century it became sociological as well, in the broadest sense of that term.

The feature of Romanticism that insists upon poetic immediacy is naturally antagonistic to the idyll as a genre; it is not surprising, therefore, to find in the Romantic poets of the nineteenth century either an absence of or an ambiguity about this form. The idyllic poet speaks from a distance, a distance that may express itself formally in a framing device, as in Theocritus, or in physical removal from the objects he discusses, as is usually the case in Gray's poems, or in the method of the dramatic monologue, where the writer describes a state of mind manifestly not his own. But the Romantic poet often wished to abolish this distance between subject and object, and insofar as this abolition was a part of the Romantic program, Romanticism attempted to restore the genuine lyrical "I" of the first melic poets in preference to the artifice of the first person singular of the idyll. This insistence upon poetic immediacy also undermined the Romantics' access to another important aspect of idyll, the manipulation of received materials. Because the Romantic, at least in one posture, wished to make a mythic statement that conformed aboslutely to the contours of his own consciousness, he was very liable not to accept received materials, but to build a personal mythology. Blake is an extreme example of this tendency, but it is also apparent in Keats's *Endymion*, in which the myth is used as a point of departure for a mythopoeia rooted not in tradition but in self.

But there was also an impulse in Romanticism toward the idyll form, and this inclination is apparent in works as diverse as Wordworth's *Michael* and Shelley's *Adonais*. The first of these is an attempt at the kind of extreme Doric realism that Theocritus brought to several of his idylls. In *Michael*, Wordsworth delineates the "domestic affections" of a country class whose "little tract of land serves as a kind of rallying point for their domestic feelings,"[20] a setting for the poem that is reminiscent of Vergil's first *Eclogue*, in which a parallel devotion to the land is portrayed as the foundation of the whole emotional network that comprises the remaining nine idylls:

> Fortunate senex, ergo tua rura manebunt,
> et tibi magna satis, quamvis lapis omnia nudus
> limosoque palus obducat pascua iunco.

Happy old man, for your land will remain your own, and that is full plenty for you, although the bare rocks and marshland with mud and reeds encroach on all your fields.

In the best idyllic tradition, *Michael* is set off by a framing device, in which the poet speaks, and these introductory lines indicate what is different about Wordsworth's use of the idyll:

> And hence this Tale, while I was yet a Boy
> Careless of books, yet having felt the power
> Of Nature, by the gentle agency
> Of natural objects, led me on to feel
> For passions that were not my own, and think
> (At random and imperfectly indeed)
> On man, the heart of man, and human life.
> Therefore, although it be a history

Homely and rude, I will relate the same
For the delight of a few natural hearts;
And, with yet fonder feeling, for the sake
Of youthful Poets, who among these hills
Will be my second self when I am gone.

The self is prominent here in a way atypical of idyll. The story of *Michael* is given as Wordsworth felt it, and so Romantic immediacy is preserved: the audience for the poem is in fact the "youthful Poets" who are Wordsworth's "second self." It was natural that Wordsworth should seek a poetry expressive of "man, the heart of man, and human life," and also natural that in reaching, as an epic poet would, toward general statements on the constitution of the universe, he should try to save the Romantic credo that the only true myth is the one that conforms to the dimensions of the poet's consciousness. What results from the attempt to combine these two strains of thought is a poetry balanced between the subjective and the objective, or, in formal terms, between lyric and idyll. By describing the history of Michael and Luke, a story he had felt deeply, Wordsworth made out of his consciousness a myth that is applicable universally. All those who also feel the impact of this history will be the poet's "second self." Thus the poet's consciousness subsumes the world, and the distinction between lyric and idyll is abolished, for the lyrical, subjective experience is finally equated with a statement of broad general truth. These principles are taken to their logical formal conclusions in *The Prelude* and *The Excursion*, where lyric and idyllic elements are worked up to epic proportions, as had been done before by Vergil, Ovid, and Milton. But in Wordsworth the self is the epic hero.

Wordsworth's idyll, then, if *Michael* may be said to represent the type, is traditional in its subject matter, its framing device, and even its sociological interests (apparent in *Michael* and more obviously in the idyllic sections of *The Excursion*), which extend the social aspects of the eighteenth-century idyll. It departs from earlier idylls in its rejection of poetic distance and literary eclecticism, or at least overt eclecticism, in the manner of Callimachus; *Michael* owes much to Vergil and the idyllic tradition, and consciously so. These idyllic elements were jettisoned in order to arrive at a direct statement of the human condition (this part of Wordsworth's idyll is traditional) that was congruent with the poet's own consciousness, and herein lay the revolution of the *Lyrical Ballads*.

Other Romantics, also eschewing received mythologies and looking for a more direct access to universal consciousness, found their answer, not in the extension of self to a general psychological principle, but in the popular forms of poetry, especially the ballad, in which the lyric "I" might speak not for the single person, but for the whole people. The ballad often seems close to the idyll form: it may take the form of a monologue, as in Scott's *Wandering Willie*, or of a mime dialogue, as in Keats's *La Belle Dame Sans Merci*. The ballad, like the idyll, describes single emotional states that are characteristic of the human condition. In its native form the ballad had lacked the self-consciousness and eclecticism of the idyll, but in the hands of the Romantics it was upgraded considerably in these respects: Coleridge's *Ancient Mariner* can surely claim to be as self-conscious and eclectic as any of the Alexandrian idylls. Under the Romantic influence the ballad also tended toward the same kind of allegory as the idyll: Keats's knight-at-arms, "alone and palely loitering," is not the tangible creature Barbara Allen is, nor is the Ancient Mariner as palpable as Patrick Spens. Both are deliberately wrought caricatures of some aspect of the psyche, as is usually the case in idyll.

The Romantics, then, did not so much discard the idyll as alter it to suit their outlook. For most of them, this alteration required a fundamental departure from the formal distance and learned machinery associated with idyll, which were replaced by aspects of the lyric. Since the idyll had always contained lyric aspects, this was not so much a change as a shift in emphasis. But in the case of Shelley, even the distancing devices and mythic features were retained. *Adonais* is a full-scale threnody on the classical models, drawing on the traditional mythic materials. Indeed, throughout his career Shelley used the classical forms in a way that in no sense rejected the tradition—the hymns to Pan and Apollo are on the model of Callimachus' hymns—but even occasionally improved it, as in *Prometheus Un-*

bound. This adherence to the received forms seems an imponderable in the most openly revolutionary of the Romantics until it is recalled that Shelley was a Platonist and believed in formal archetypes. *Adonais* was written as a pastoral elegy like Theocritus' *Daphnis* or Moschus' *Lament for Bion,* because this for Shelley was the form that perfectly embodied the aspect of eternal truth latent in any poetic discussion of death. In this as in other respects Shelley was a neoclassicist, and a more thorough one than Pope: "The one remains, the many change and pass," a dictum apparently true of literary forms as well as spirits. Shelley respected the tradition from which Tennyson developed his concept of idyll as an archetypal model of formal truth.

THREE

Tennyson's Early Poetry and the Idyllic Tradition

THE ALEXANDRIAN TRADITION from which Tennyson's concept of idyll developed was subtle and complex, and it became even more so during the century preceding his birth. It would be a grave mistake to tax Tennyson with simplemindedness or poetic sloth for having chosen to work primarily in the idyllic vein. And choose to work in it he certainly did. His published and unpublished work up to 1832 shows that he experimented with a number of poetic forms as he sought to match his vision to a suitable medium, but it is apparent that early in his career he settled on the idyll as a favored method of expression. He seems to have chosen it purposely as the form out of which the larger, more bardic creations would naturally flow: *The Palace of Art* is a conscious statement of this formal program. Tennyson's drift toward the idyll is evident both in the formal direction of his early work and in his own appreciation of this direction as expressed in the arrangement of the published body of his verse.

At first glance it is difficult to draw from Tennyson's early work any definite conclusions about the nature of his poetry. It is clearly experimental, employing a wide variety of forms, but most of these he used less and less frequently, in their pure manifestations, as he settled upon his own interpretation of idyll and made it his characteristic medium. Naturally, these early poems included attempts in the lyric form, such as the imitation of Horace, *Did Not Thy*

Roseate Lips Outlive (1827), and later, *Claribel* (1830).
But the lyric was never a comfortable form for Tennyson,
and although his more mature work contains many lyric
elements, genuine lyric poetry was a rarity with him. In his
early verse he tried the formal ode a number of times, as in
Sublimity (1827), *Time: An Ode* (1827), the *Ode to Memory* (1830), and *O Bosky Brook* (which was not published
during his lifetime). There is even a mock ode, *I Dare Not
Write an Ode for Fear Pimplaea* (also not published in his
lifetime), in which he feigns dismay at the prospect of producing poetry that could survive the criticism of the day or
the charge of imitation:

> But ah! my hopes are all as dead as mutton,
>   As vain as Catholick Emancipation,
> E'en now my conscience pulls me by the button
>   And bids me cease to prate of imitation.
> What countless ills a minor bard environ—
> "*You're imitating Whistlecraft and Byron.*" (31–36)

I Dare Not Write an Ode is itself an ode, and its mock dismay is curiously acute, for Tennyson faced the same kind of
anxiety that had been one of the impulses behind the Hellenistic idyll: the belief that all the great things had been
done in poetry.[1] As the mock ode shows, Tennyson was
willing to tackle the classical forms even while he pondered
how to get beyond the tradition. But the ode was not to be
the formal vehicle for this leap.

A similar process of formal experimentation is apparent
in his early use of the sonnet. Tennyson clearly was not
comfortable in this form either ("I never care to read a
perfect sonnet," he told Allingham in 1880, "I look down
the rhymes and that's enough"),[2] but in the volume of 1830,
next to his several attempts in the form, there are *Love, Love
and Death*, and *The Kraken*, which are quasi-sonnets. The
Kraken, for instance, is fifteen, not fourteen, lines long, and
would be a normal, if slightly irregular sonnet (its octave
is a mixture of the Italian and Shakespearean rhyme
schemes) except that the neatly connected rhyme collapses
in the thirteenth line, where the formal structure of a sonnet is abandoned:

Below the thunders of the upper deep;
Far, far beneath the abysmal sea,
His ancient, dreamless, uninvaded sleep
The Kraken sleepeth: faintest sunlights flee
About his shadowy sides: above him swell
Huge sponges of millennial growth and height;
And far away into the sickly light,
From many a wondrous grot and secret cell
Unnumber'd and enormous polypi
Winnow with giant arms the slumbering green.
There hath he lain for ages and will lie .
Battening upon huge seaworms in his sleep,
Until the latter fire shall heat the deep;
Then once by man and angels to be seen,
In roaring he shall rise and on the surface die.

The line describing the apocalypse, is, of course, the appropriate place to surrender the formal rigidity of the sonnet structure—here the rhyme sends the reader back to the first line, thereby encompassing and closing off the body of the poem, as the apolcalypse does the created world. *The Kraken*, in fact, like *I Dare Not Write an Ode*, is indicative of a willingness to push past the classical models in playful and innovative ways.

Comparable experiments can be found elsewhere in the early poetry. When he was about thirteen, Tennyson translated the first lines of Claudian's *De Raptu Proserpinae* in heroic couplets. *The Devil and the Lady*, written when he was fifteen, is a verse drama that plays on Elizabethan, Jacobean, and Byronic traditions. Of special interest to Tennyson were metrical and rhyming experiments, embodied in *Leonine Elegiacs* (1830), *Anacreontics* (1830), *Elegiacs* (not published in Tennyson's lifetime), and others, in which he attempted the very difficult task of incorporating the accents and quantities of classical verse into the English system of stress and rhyme. But while all these efforts possess curiosity value as early imitative sketches of a great artist, none of them prepares us for the distinctive Tennysonian form that was to emerge from them.

It is tempting to treat this diverse body of early work as having only a thematic unity, and to approach the essential Tennyson in terms of his thought instead of his craftsmanship. There is, certainly, great thematic agreement between the work of the young and the old Tennyson: the apocalyptic vision of *Timbuctoo* (1829), the divided mentality that finds expression in companion pieces such as *All Things Will Die* and *Nothing Will Die* (1830), the fascination with a palpable nature rooted in time, and the certainty that time and matter must vanish in eternity—all these concepts, which dominate the mature poetry, are present in some shape in the early work. Even the Arthurian obsession is present in *The Lady of Shalott* (1832). Thematically, Tennyson's poetry offers an almost banal unity, for the complexion of his thought did not so much change, or even evolve, as it deepened and put down roots:

> in the light of great eternity
> Life eminent creates the shade of death;
> The shadow passeth when the tree shall fall,
> But I shall reign for ever over all.

Spirit, nearing yon dark portal at the limit of thy human
    state,
Fear not thou the hidden purpose of that Power which alone
    is great,
Nor the myriad world, His shadow, nor the silent Opener
    of the Gate.

These very similar reflections on death are separated by more than sixty years—the first is Love speaking in *Love and Death* (1830), the second is a voice of consolation from across the bar in *God and the Universe* (1892). But formally there is a great deal of difference between these two passages. The earlier is in straightforward iambic pentameter with a sonnetlike rhyme scheme capped by a couplet. The later is couched in Tennyson's majestic trochees (the hemistich before the caesura is pure trochaic; but once the meter has been established, anapests appear in the rest of the line), and artistic cunning is seemingly abandoned by employing a triple rhyme, which makes the stanza seem both massive and obvious. This effect is further enhanced by the heavy beat of the trochees and the extent of the line—it has eight feet, approaching the limit of the number a reader can hear, and still perceive the line as a unit. Compared with the singsong quality of *Love and Death, God and the Universe* is a technical masterpiece, a triumph of poetic craft masquerading as simplicity. If God were to speak, He would undoubtedly choose this trochaic mode of expression. While there is then thematic agreement between the early and the mature poetry of Tennyson, there is, more significantly, progress and evolution in his use of form and technique; and viewed in this light, the early poetry can be treated as experimental exercises built around certain fixed themes. We will look in vain for evidence of the maturation of Tennyson's thought if we separate content from form in his poetry, for Tennyson's growth as a poet took place not in what he had to say, but in how he said it. When read aright, the history of his manipulation of form is the history of his mind.

Tennyson himself regarded his early poetry as formally experimental, and he did not wish the general public to see very many of his youthful exercises. (Christopher Ricks's edition makes available in one place a large number of youthful poems that Tennyson never published.) Also revealing of the poet's attitude toward his early pieces is the way in which he dealt with those that he included in the canon in editions of his work published from 1842 onward. Like Wordsworth's arrangement of his own collected works, Tennyson's mature positioning of his poetry is a critical statement in its own right and must not be ignored, for it shows both what Tennyson thought was good in his own work and how he thought the work fitted together.[3]

As long as he lived, Tennyson played with the selection and arrangement of poems in editions of his collected work. The two volumes of 1842, published under the collective title *Poems*, are the first example of this. In them, Tennyson presented new verse from the period 1832–1842 (the famous "ten years' silence"), during which he had written much but published no new volume. But Volume One of *Poems* was also a new edition of his early work, an anthology of what he considered his best pieces, many of them in highly revised forms. Subsequent editions of his collected poetry further demonstrate the Tennysonian procedures of selection and revision: the early poetry was carefully weeded and assigned to various divisions; verses considered good but flawed appeared as "Juvenilia"; and the "mature" works were eventually headed by a division entitled *"The Lady of Shalott* and Other Poems." (Maturity was a qualitative, not a chronological, concept for Tennyson, and the word is used here in his sense.) This study refers to six editions or collections of Tennyson's poetry, all published under his editorial supervision, in order to demonstrate how his critical judgments about his work reveal his sense of the poetry's function and purpose. These editions are the one of 1832, containing the core of poems around which he invariably built the first division of mature verse; the *Poems* of 1842; and the omnibus volumes of 1857, 1884, 1890, and 1892, all of which show important changes in arrangement and selection.

In these editions, it is interesting to note not only what Tennyson included or revised, but what he omitted. For instance, nothing from the 1827 volume, *Poems by Two Brothers*, was reprinted by Tennyson, and the Cambridge prize poem, *Timbuctoo* (1829), was not permitted in the canon of his work while he lived, in spite of its favorable reception. (It not only won the prize, but it was also well received outside Cambridge; the *Athenaeum* wrote that it was a poem that indicated a "first-rate poetical genius, and which would have done honour to any man that ever wrote.") This would seem to indicate that Tennyson was less swayed by criticism, both good and bad, in weeding out his early verse than has been assumed, and that he used some other principle in selecting poems for his collected works.[4]

That this principle of selection was a rigorous one can be seen in the way the mature Tennyson treated his volumes of 1830 and 1832. A number of poems were relegated to the same obscurity as the entire 1827 volume; those that were suffered to reappear in the 1842 and later editions did so under the heading Juvenilia or in greatly revised versions. In his use of the word Juvenilia, Tennyson defined the work of his youth very broadly, for the poetry falling under this classification had all been published, if not written, when he was between twenty-one and twenty-three. (By the same standard, *Endymion* and the sonnet *To One Who Has Been Long in City Pent*, along with the letter on "Negative

Capability," would belong among Keats's juvenilia.) Also, some of the poems that Tennyson grouped as juvenilia are among his best-known works: *The Kraken, Mariana, Supposed Confessions of a Second-rate Sensitive Mind,* and *Recollections of the Arabian Nights.* True, adverse criticism undoubtedly did prompt Tennyson to delete some poems from his collected poetry and to demote others to the status of juvenilia: J. W. Crocker's violent attack on *O Darling Room,* for instance, seems to have been sufficient to cause Tennyson to eradicate the lyric from all future editions of his work, as well as to instill in him a profound wariness of the word "darling," which he systematically expunged from some of his verse.[5] But why *The Hesperides* should have disappeared completely while *The Miller's Daughter,* in revised form, was admitted to the main body of collected works is baffling at first sight. And why did he relegate *Mariana* to the juvenilia while publishing *The Lady of Shalott* among the supposedly mature works?

The answers lie in Tennyson's gradual progress toward a form of poetry that he considered appropriate to the poetic statement he wished to make, the form that he conceived as idyll. Ever since his early poetic attempt to translate Claudian's *De Raptu Proserpinae,* the fifth-century poem that continues the Hellenistic tradition by recreating ancient myth and its epic pretensions, Tennyson had shown an abiding interest in the form evolved by the Alexandrians and its different poetic manifestations. Indeed, Tennyson's poetic career is a history of the idyll in miniature: his poetry begins, like that of the Alexandrians, by being acutely self-conscious and eclectic; it develops a certain self-assurance and confidence that allows it to be simpler and more direct than the earlier experiments in the style of Callimachus; and finally, as had occurred with Vergil and Ovid, it gains the confidence to fulfill its epic inclinations in *The Idylls of the King.* The first stages of this history are evident in Tennyson's early verse and his arrangement of that verse in the collected editions of his work.

By the time the poetry that Tennyson regarded as polished enough to stand on its own without the label juvenilia appeared, the range of forms he employed had narrowed significantly. The early sonnets were placed among the juvenilia; the early odes, with the exception of the *Ode to Memory* with its important statement on his theory of forms, were excluded. Lyric poetry, if lyric is defined as a form in which the "I" of the poem and the poet are taken to be interchangeable, was represented by no more than four selections out of the twenty-two that formed the first division of his works, "*The Lady of Shalott* and Other Poems." What remained was a fairly homogeneous collection of verse that tended toward idyll, just as the stanza schemes and meters of the poetry tended toward simplicity. (J. F. Pyre noted that the early poems discarded by Tennyson were, almost invariably, metrically complex or schematically ornate; it follows that if he was searching for means of expression that were, at least on their surface, simple, he would have been naturally attracted to the idyll.)[6] What Tennyson's early work contributed to the development of his own concept of the idyll can be shown by considering the first few poems that he ranked among his adult craftsmanship: the first four poems in Tennyson's mature recension of his early work, "*The Lady of Shalott* and Other Poems."

The Lady of Shalott, which Tennyson placed first, offers a particularly good example of the formal properties that most attracted him. Like many of the early works, *The Lady of Shalott* draws on fairly recondite material; according to Tennyson, its source was the late-thirteenth-century Italian story, *Qui conta come la Damigella di Scalot mori per amore di Lancialotto.*[7] But as commentators have pointed out, Tennyson's treatment of the Lady is very different from the original: he added the Arthurian background, invented the Lady's island home, and introduced the mirror, the curse, and the weaving. This, of course, is the usual pattern in the idyll, where, in the epyllion tradition (the *Lady of Shalott* is an epyllion drawing on Arthurian legend instead of Homeric myth), received materials are altered to suit the dictates of the new form. It is interesting to note not only what Tennyson added to the story, but also what he omitted. Like the Hellenistic treatment of Homeric myth, Tennyson's treatment of the Lady isolates her from any continuous narrative flow. The plot structure of *La Damigella di Scalot,* which, though short, tells of the Lady's love for Lancelot, his rejection of her, and her letter, is discarded in favor of a succession of images, just as Theocritus rejected the plot surrounding the Cyclops and focused on Polyphemus' emotions. Similarly, by sacrificing plot, Tennyson makes the now nebulous Lady and her interior world the center of attention. As with all idylls, the accenting of a single character who is indicative of some psychic condition, rather than the stressing of narrative continuity, shifts the poem toward allegory. It was hardly accidental that the source from which Tennyson derived two of the features he added to his Italian source—the mirror and Lancelot's appearance—was the great English allegory, *The Faerie Queene*.

But while *The Lady of Shalott* clearly indulges in allegory of some sort, it is not precisely of the Spenserian type. In *The Faerie Queene*, plot, names, allusions, and iconography assist the reader in arriving at an understanding of what the allegory represents; in *The Lady of Shalott*, these aids are gone. The plot is dismantled; the Lady's name is used only for its sound, not its significance— "Shalott" was softer than "Scalott," Tennyson said;[8] there are no learned references or allusions in the text; and the iconography of the poem little resembles Spenser's or, say, that of the Unicorn Tapestries, where every descriptive element is meant to trigger an association of ideas.

What remains, and what gives rise to allegory, is character. The Lady, surrounded by a great deal of well-lit physical imagery, is indicative of an obscure and disembodied psychic state. She is cursed to live in the mirror's world of reflected images and in the shadow of the living world that surrounds her:

> Or when the moon was overhead,
> Came two young lovers lately wed;
> "I am half sick of shadows," said
>   The Lady of Shalott.   (69–72)

In his review of the earlier *Poems Chiefly Lyrical* (1830) Arthur Hallam described the process employed by Tennyson in *The Lady of Shalott*:

Mr. Tennyson's way of proceeding seems to be this. He collects the most striking phenomena of individual minds until he arrives at some leading fact, which allows him to lay down an axiom or law; and then, working on the law thus attained, he clearly discerns the tendency of what new particulars his invention suggests, and is enabled to impress an individual freshness and unity on ideal combinations. These expressions of character are brief and coherent; nothing extraneous to the dominant fact is admitted, nothing illustrative of it, and, as it were, growing out of it, is rejected. They are like summaries of mighty dramas. We do not say this method admits of such large luxuriance of power as that of our real dramatists; but we contend that it is a new species of poetry, a graft of the lyric on the dramatic, and Mr. Tennyson deserves the laurel of an inventor, an enlarger of our modes of knowledge and power.[9]

While Hallam's observations on Tennyson's method in these early poems are very much to the point, his claim that Tennyson "deserves the laurel of an inventor" is perhaps a bit grandiose. At this time in his career Tennyson was not discovering new forms but rediscovering an old one, the idyll. The combination of the lyric and dramatic had already been used by the Alexandrian poets to depict isolated psychological states objectively studied. *The Lady of Shalott* examines one part of the universe of the psyche in a form that, while it partakes of both the ancient and Romantic forms of the lyric (the poem employs the first person for the Lady and is cast in a quasi-ballad mode),[10] is more clinical than lyric, and that, while dramatic, nonetheless provides a static, enduring portrait of one emotional condition beyond the confines of the drama's plot and movement.

The one emotional condition described by *The Lady of Shalott* is purposely made general; perhaps it can best be called melancholia. The state in which the Lady suffers is not precisely lovesickness, for Tennyson has carefully abstracted her from the romantic plot surrounding her in his sources; nor can it be said with certainty that she suffers from an artist's melancholy, though it is perfectly possible to read the poem in either way—as a Freudian study of imprisoned libido wilting away to death or as a Jungian allegory of the anima, turning away from its inner creativity only to be crushed in its confrontation with reality.[11] Both readings are valid, but both proceed from the poem's primary achievement, an objective, idyllic description of a general psychological state of melancholy. Both the Freudian and

Jungian readings of the poem imply a moral interpretation: either it is bad to suppress one's libido, and if you do, you die; or it is bad to subject the creative imagination to the limitations of the real world, and if you do, it dies. Tennyson's own portrait of the Lady, broader than either of these narrow interpretations, is left without moral perspective, which is the neutral stance of the idyll. What Tennyson is describing in the Lady may be, like Epicharmus' work, "useful," but it is not didactic. With the Lady, Tennyson begins to create idyllic descriptions that transcend morality in their aim of achieving minutely accurate studies of the human personality.

The Lady of Shalott, then, is an idyll, almost an epyllion, concentrating on but radically altering one aspect of received lore, *La Damigella di Scalot*. It is, in the idyll tradition, allegorical, but its allegory is purposely nebulous in order that its application may be broad. This statement of a general psychic condition is facilitated by casting the poem in the universal form of the ballad. Through all this, the poet himself is removed from the context of the poem, maintaining the distance typical of Hellenistic poetry.

The progression out of lyric and toward the objective description of universal states is again exemplified in *Fatima*, which in the 1832 volume was entitled from its first words ("O Love, Love, Love") and headed by two lines from Sappho,

φαίνεταί μοι κῆνος ἶσος θέοσιν
ἔμμεν ὤνηρ,

the first lines of Sappho's second fragment ("That man seems to me equal to the gods"), introducing one of her most fervid love lyrics. Here, Tennyson makes the poem's lyric origin explicit by the Sapphic epigraph, which is echoed in the text when he quotes further from Sappho's poem:

Last night, when some one spoke his name
From my swift blood that went and came
A thousand little shafts of flame
Were shivered in my narrow frame.   (15–18)

This is, of course, a translation not only of Sappho, but of Theocritus' adaptation of Sappho in his second idyll, *The Spell*. In fact, Tennyson is doing with Sappho exactly what Theocritus had done; he is taking lyric material and converting it to descriptive, psychological purposes. *Fatima*, like Theocritus' *Spell*, is a dramatic monologue portraying a woman's frustrated sexual passion. (Theocritus' second idyll was a favorite with Tennyson; he used it extensively in *Oenone* as well.) As the titles show, Tennyson had experimented widely with the monologue form inherited from the Alexandrians: the 1827 volume contained *Antony to Cleopatra, Mithradates Presenting Berenice with the Cup of Poison, Lamentation of the Peruvians, The High-Priest to Alexander, The Dying Man to his Friend* (in imitation of Pope's *Dying Christian*), and, in the tradition of Gray's *Bard* and Scott's *The Bard's Incantation, The Druid's Prophecies*. Tennyson was obviously familiar with the monologue as a technique for presenting mental attitudes and states, but when he came to select the monologues to be incorporated in his collected works as adult poems, he eschewed the grand, historical subjects like Antony and Cleopatra or the last Druid in favor of the disembodied voice of the lovelorn Fatima—who until 1842 was so disembodied as not to possess a name—or of the mythical monologue, which constitutes the epyllion *Oenone*. The direction Tennyson was indicating for his poetry in these choices is clear: he was aiming for the universal psychological statements provided by allegory and myth rather than for any concrete, historical context. In *Fatima*, this is further confirmed by his manipulation of his source: the story of Fatima is derived, says W. D. Paden, from Savary's *Letters on Egypt*, where the lady is a married woman whose lover fears to come to her by night because of her husband. All hint of this plot disappears in Tennyson. Aside from verbal echoes of the original (lines 11 and 12 of the poem are taken directly from Savary), what remains is the essence of a woman in the throes of a grand passion. Tennyson has transformed the concrete into the universal.

Oenone is the companion piece of *Fatima;* Tennyson always had them printed next to each other, like *Isabel* and *Mariana*. Both are love laments. *Fatima* is worked out in

ballad form; *Oenone*, which is a true epyllion, draws on
the mythic tradition and appears in blank verse, Tennyson's
answer to the Alexandrian hexameters of the Hellenistic
epyllion. Although, both draw heavily on the same Theocritean idyll, *The Spell*, in *Oenone* Tennyson not only is
working in a loftier vein than the ballad form, but is presenting his allegory in a more complex setting. *Fatima* is a
rendering of the soul laboring under a grand passion; *Oenone*
is also that, but more. She tells not only of her sorrow in
losing Paris to Helen, but recounts the Judgment of Paris.
Oenone's monologue is set before the start of the Trojan
War, so that she is not yet aware how completely the world
will come to share her grief over Paris' choice. She describes how Hera offers Paris power, "Which in all action
is the end of all" (120); Athena tops this bid by offering
"Self-reverence, self-knowledge, self-control, / These three
alone lead life to sovereign power" (142–143). Aphrodite's
offer of love is, by comparison with the ornate rhetoric of
Hera and Athena, succinct and sure of purpose. Her whole
speech is, "I promise thee / The fairest and most loving
wife in Greece" (182–183). Paris instantly accepts.

The Judgment of Paris was a favorite neoclassical subject, and Tennyson seems here to be working closely from
both the Hellenistic models and the seventeenth- and
eighteenth-century canvases. (Van Dyke had produced a
famous Judgment of Paris, as had Watteau and Rubens.)
In comparison with the freshness and mystery that surround
the Lady of Shalott and Fatima, Oenone appears to be a
stodgy character, and her poem is certainly full of rhetoric
and classical device.[12] But Tennyson is busily at work in
Oenone practicing his use of idyll and the allegory concomitant with it: having presented the allegory of Power,
Knowledge, and Beauty in neoclassical strokes, he returns
the idyll to its proper psychological sphere in its final, best
lines:

> I will rise and go
> Down into Troy, and ere the stars come forth
> Talk with the wild Cassandra, for she says
> A fire dances before her, and a sound

Rings ever in her ears of armèd men.
What this may be I know not, but I know
That, wheresoe'er I am by night and day,
All earth and air seem only burning fire.   (257–264)

The Homeric fires that will consume Troy are secondary to the Theocritean flames that devour Oenone; the human heart is primary, and action proceeds from it. The traditional allegorical representations of Hera, Athena, and Aphrodite are too staid and one-dimensional; the mood and passion of the heart, here expressed (as it is traditionally) in terms of flame, supersedes them all. *Oenone* is Tennyson's attempt to meld the classical idyll style of mythic tableaux with the new, ballad-style, psychological examination he had practiced in *Fatima*. The blending of these two forms of idyll will be a continuing preoccupation in his verse, achieving its formal balance in his later poetry.

The Miller's Daughter explores yet another aspect of the idyllic genre. Like the poems surrounding it in the volume of 1832 (it was heavily revised for inclusion in the 1842 edition), it is about love, and like *Fatima*, which immediately followed it, it is a monologue. But the "late-left orphan of the squire" who narrates the simple story of falling in love with Alice, the miller's daughter, wooing her, marrying her, and living pastorally ever after, has a happy tale to relate:

Have I not found a happy earth?
    I least should breathe a thought of pain.
Would God renew me from my birth
    I'd almost live my life again.
So sweet it seems with thee to walk,
    And once again to woo thee mine—
It seems in after-dinner talk
    Across the walnuts and the wine.   (25–32)

This domestic idyll is a portrait of the realm where Tithonus longs to dwell, among "the homes / Of happy men that have the power to die." It is too often overlooked that Tennyson wrote about tranquil psychological states as well as morbid ones. *The Miller's Daughter* is an idyll like Theocritus' *Harvest Home* (Idyll VII) or the pastoral-idyllic novels that grew out of the Hellenistic tradition, and it frankly delights in nature. It places the birth of love in springtime and treats visible nature and human nature as analogues, both subject to a wholly beneficent cycle of growth and decay. Even the death of his son is gratefully accepted by the narrator, since "that loss but made us love the more" (230). Alice and the narrator age together and placidly await death as the natural and happy conclusion of their quiet lives:

> Arise, and let us wander forth,
>   To yon old mill across the wolds;
> For look, the sunset, south and north,
>   Winds all the vale in rosy folds,
> And fires your narrow casement glass,
>   Touching the sullen pool below;
> On the chalk-hill the bearded grass
>   Is dry and dewless. Let us go.   (239–246)

The setting sun still lights the "sullen pool," the same pool in which he first saw his wife as "the reflex of a beauteous form" when, "an absent fool," he fished as a young man (60–80). Nature is a perfect, luminescent continuity, equally beautifying youth and age.

The Miller's Daughter is also a monologue and should not be treated as a direct statement of Tennyson's sentiments any more than other idyll forms from the 1832 volume should be treated as personal or lyric statements. The piece seems to be present in Tenyson's canon to lend a balance to the early poems—it is balancing in both its calm and its use of an idyllic genre that can accommodate plot and narration. Although Tennyson's decision in 1842 to keep *The Miller's Daughter* when he reissued the bulk of the poems of 1832 and to exclude the now acclaimed *Hesperides* seems puzzling today, it is understandable on several counts. *The Hesperides* is an inchoate dramatic monologue sung with one voice by the daughters of Hesperus—its very inchoateness makes it attractive in this century; its mood and its format are so similar to *The Lotus-Eaters*, which followed it in the 1832 edition, that it would have been redundant if Tennyson was thinking of his poems as part of a developing pattern; and it had overloaded the balance of the 1832 poems in the direction of the morbid and depressed.[13] In addition, *The Hesperides* contains a great deal of the luxuriant wording that Tennyson systematically removed in his later poetry—expressions like "bloombright," "cedarshade," and "lotusflute"—and it is in a complex meter and rhyme, whereas elsewhere the poet was moving toward balladlike simplicity.

Tennyson, in fact, seems to have taken great pains with the order and balance of poems in each of the divisions he assigned to his published work. This was a natural outcome of working in the idyll form, which invites the building of connections between its various separate statements, as in Vergil's *Eclogues*. That Tennyson was aiming at some kind of cohesion for his early poems was shown by the effort he expended on their arrangements in every edition of his collected works. The order he gave the first series of poems of the 1832 volume in their later manifestations illuminates this point. The list on page 56 shows how they were arranged in 1832, 1842, 1857, 1884, 1890, and 1892; titles not listed after 1832 were relegated to the Juvenilia section of his works or discarded altogether.

To the end of his life, Tennyson was trying to put the early poems into a unifying pattern. In these paratactical exercises, he eliminated any connection between the *Lady of Shalott* and the poems that had originally preceded it, placing them in a separate section. The remaining early poems he then attempted to harmonize in theme and form.

Mariana in the South continues the theme of *The Lady of Shalott*, which depicts the psyche as it confronts itself and the external world and conveys the prevailing tone of melancholy. In a way that the earlier *Mariana* (1830) could not have done, *Mariana in the South* builds upon this theme by picking up much of the imagery of *The Lady of Shalott*, such as the Lady's mirror: "And on the liquid mirror glowed / The clear perfection of her face" (31–32). The world of flux so prominent in *The Lady of Shalott* also surrounds *Mariana in the South:*

TENNYSON'S ARRANGEMENT OF HIS EARLY POEMS IN
VARIOUS EDITIONS OF HIS WORK

1832

Sonnet, Mine be the strength
To———
Buonaparte
Sonnet
The Lady of Shalott
Mariana in the South
Eleänore
The Miller's Daughter
Fatima
Oenone
The Sisters
To———, With the Follow-
  ing Poem
The Palace of Art

1842

The Lady of Shalott
Mariana in the South
Eleänore
The Miller's Daughter
Fatima
Oenone
The Sisters
To———, With the Follow-
  ing Poem
The Palace of Art

1857

The Lady of Shalott
Eleänore
Mariana in the South
The Miller's Daughter
Fatima
Oenone
The Sisters
To———, With the Follow-
  ing Poem
The Palace of Art

1884

The Lady of Shalott
The Two Voices
The Miller's Daughter
Fatima
Oenone
The Sisters
To———, With the Follow-
  ing Poem
The Palace of Art

1890

The Two Voices
The Miller's Daughter
Fatima
Oenone
The Sisters
To———, With the Follow-
  ing Poem
The Palace of Art

1892

The Lady of Shalott
Mariana in the South
The Two Voices
The Miller's Daughter
Fatima
Oenone
The Sisters
To———, With the Follow-
  ing Poem
The Palace of Art

But sometimes in the falling day
   An image seemed to pass the door,
To look into her face and say,
   "But thou shalt be alone no more."
And flaming downward over all
   From heat to heat the day decreased,
And slowly rounded to the east
   The one black shadow from the wall.
     "The day to night," she made her moan,
     "The day to night, the night to morn,
   And day and night I am left alone
     To live forgotten, and love forlorn."   (73–84)

Like the Lady, Mariana dwells in a world of images; she is haunted by the image of her lover as the Lady was by Lancelot's reflection in the mirror. Unlike the character of the original *Mariana*, who lived in a world of bitter realities and wished to die, Mariana in the South (like the Lady) inhabits a twilight world where illusion and reality blend, and she wishes to live, praying to the Virgin to give her strength.

But if *Mariana in the South* was designed to continue the themes established in *The Lady of Shalott*, it was open to the charge of doing so too closely. The Lady and Mariana are perhaps too similar to form a progression, and sensing this, Tennyson in 1884 omitted it from the opening series of poems in *The Lady of Shalott* division of his works. A similar objection explains why *Eleänore* was assigned to the Juvenilia section of the same edition: the poem is the lament of its narrator for the love of Eleänore, and its presence at the beginning of this division of the poetry tips the balance too much toward the love lament. The free stanza form of *Eleänore* is also reminiscent of the ode structure that Tennyson was at pains to eliminate from this section of his poetry. It is not surprising, therefore, that it stayed in the Juvenilia in subsequent editions.

The Miller's Daughter provided both continuity and emotional balance where Tennyson positioned it in the series of his early poems. The prominent description of physical reality used as a counterpart to the inner state of the central figure, a method apparent in *The Lady of*

Shalott and *Mariana in the South*, is continued here, right down to the mirror image, which recurs when the narrator sees the image of his bride-to-be in the pond where he is fishing: "The reflex of a beauteous form, / a glowing arm, a gleaming neck" (77–78). But in this poem the image is not irreconcilable with life in the material world: in *The Miller's Daughter* the longing, that animates the Lady and Mariana, for the fulfillment of disembodied desire in the realm of the concrete is actually achieved in a pastoral, domestic idyll. The possibility of this realization was of great importance to Tennyson, and *The Miller's Daughter* was never removed from this series of poems, finally taking its place in 1892 as the culminating pastoral vision toward which the first poems move.

To replace the ode-like *Eleänore* in the series leading up to the happy statement of *The Miller's Daughter*, Tennyson finally nominated *The Two Voices*. A fitting choice, *The Two Voices* is a prolonged investigation of the state of melancholy that has afflicted the Lady and Mariana, and it is formulated in yet another kind of idyll, amoeban verse. In the original amoeban form, two shepherds exchanged verses, capping each other in a pastoral contest. Vergil's seventh eclogue is an example of the type, which was often changed by Christian writers into a debate between body and soul, as in Marvell's *Dialogue between the Soul and Body*. Tennyson took the amoeban form one step further and turned it into an interior debate between the logic of despair and the assertion of hope. The mirror imagery that had filled the first two poems in this series is carried forward in the voice of despair's discussion of the illusory nature of man in the world:

> That type of Perfect in his mind
> In Nature can he nowhere find.
> He sows himself on every wind.
>
> . . . . .
>
> Heaven opens inward, chasms yawn,
> Vast images in glimmering dawn,
> Half-shown, are broken and withdrawn.
>
> (292–294, 304–306)

The voice of hope finally overcomes the arguments of despair that assail the narrator as they have assailed and possessed the Lady of Shalott and Mariana, and his cheer, after exorcising the spirit of despair, neatly prepares the reader for the domestic idyll of *The Miller's Daughter*, which immediately follows. From his window, the narrator of *The Two Voices* sees a family scene—husband, wife, child:

> The prudent partner of his blood
> Leaned on him, faithful, gentle, good,
> Wearing the rose of womanhood.
>
> And in their double love secure,
> The little maiden walked demure,
> Pacing with downward eyelids pure.
> These three made unity so sweet
> My frozen heart began to beat,
> Remembering its ancient heat.   (415–424)

The way has been cleared for an easy transition from the internal amoeban verse form to the pastoral idyll; it is not surprising that several of the lines Tennyson rejected for *The Miller's Daughter* found their way, in altered form, into *The Two Voices*.[14] In fact, the two poems taken together so well express the conflicting psychic states that Tennyson aimed to portray in this series that he omitted *The Lady of Shalott* and *Mariana in the South* from the 1890 volume of his works and let *The Two Voices* stand at the beginning of this section, followed by *The Miller's Daughter*.

If the first poems in "*The Lady of Shalott* and Other Poems" section of Tennyson's work all focus on a single mental state, exploring its different aspects in different forms of idyll, the next few poems, culminating in *The Palace of Art*, also have continuity, both one with another and with *The Lady of Shalott, Mariana in the South, The Two Voices*, and *The Miller's Daughter*.

In *The Palace of Art* the tendency toward allegory observable in *Fatima, The Lady of Shalott*, and *The Two Voices* culminates in a full-scale, traditional, allegorical treatment. As Tennyson wrote of it in the dedicatory poem to R. C. Trench that prefaces *The Palace of Art*,

I send you here a sort of allegory,
(For you will understand it) of a soul,
A sinful soul possessed of many gifts,
A spacious garden full of flowering weeds,
A glorious Devil, large in heart and brain,
That did love Beauty only, (Beauty seen
In all varieties of mould and mind)
And Knowledge for its beauty; or if Good,
Good only for its beauty, seeing not
That Beauty, Good, and Knowledge, are three sisters
That doat upon each other.   (1–11)

The piece fits neatly into the thematic context of the other poems. It and its introductory lines, *To———, With the Following Poem*, were preceded in all of Tennyson's editions by *The Sisters*, a ballad of revenge wrought by one sister for the shameful death of the other, just as the "sister" virtues of *The Palace of Art* revenge one another; and *Oenone* has also described Paris' ill-fated choice between the goddesses representing three cardinal virtues. *The Palace of Art* is a more elaborate treatment of an allegorical theme well established in the early poems of the 1832 volume. But it is only "a sort of allegory"; like *The Lady of Shalott*, it lacks the fixed equivalencies between tenor and vehicle that mark medieval and Renaissance allegory. Like the majority of the 1832 poems, *The Palace of Art* is, in the idyllic tradition, carefully dissociated from Tennyson's own personality, both by the prefatory poem (the allegory is of "A sinful soul," not particularly Tennyson's) and by the structure of the poem, which creates a vague "I" narrator and then moves away from him to a description of the Soul: Tennyson is twice removed from the narrative.[15]

The psychic condition into which the Soul has fallen in *The Palace of Art* is akin to that of the Lady of Shalott: both are latter-day representations of melancholy, set apart in immured and towered environments and contemplating the word only in images. The Soul of *The Palace of Art* adds to the portrait of the Lady of Shalott the element of pride, which leads her to announce, just before she is "struck through with pangs of hell,"

I take possession of man's mind and deed.
I care not what the sects may brawl.
I sit as God holding no form of creed,
But contemplating all.[16]   (209–212)

The Soul had hoped, through art, to encompass all things—
in heaven and earth, past and present. She has epic ambitions,
like Tennyson and the idyll form.

Throughout his poetic career, Tennyson was strongly
attracted to the doctrine he puts into the sinful Soul's mouth;
this doctrine is a species of pantheism, which holds that the
universe is encompassed by a single thing or principle synonymous with God. Such a doctrine would have far-
reaching repercussions for a poet like Tennyson whose art
revolved around the manipulation of form. In *The Palace
of Art* he comes to grips with this theory and also with his
own formal direction in his early poems. If he believed in
pantheism literally, as the Soul of the poem does, then all
forms, both material shapes and mental structures, including
poetic genres, would be illusory boundaries imposed by the
corrupt mind of man and segmenting a universe that is truly
at unity. This in crude terms was Blake's position, and it is
the Soul's when she announces that she "holds no form of
creeds" but sees all.

For Tennyson, however, no matter how attractive this
view seemed, it was untenable: to be a true pantheist, one
must disbelieve in God as distinct from humankind and
human history (which the Soul does—"I sit as God").
Tennyson could not believe this. Also, the pantheist regards
the concepts of morality and progress with a bemused dis-
dain nicely captured in Fitzgerald's translation of the
Rubaiyat:

And if the Wine you drink, the Lip you press,
End in what All begins and ends in—Yes;
    Think that you are Today what Yesterday
You were—Tomorrow you shall not be less. (165–168)

Tennyson was not prepared to regard either time or morality
as illusory, but he was also not ready to abandon the attrac-

tive core of pantheism that finds mystic unity in all time and matter. When he was sixty, he wrote in *The Higher Pantheism*, "Dark is the world to thee: and thou fulfillest thy doom, / Making Him broken gleams, and stifled splendour and gloom." Tennyson's position was essentially the young Newman's, that there are "two and two only absolute and luminously self-evident beings, myself and my Creator."[17] But these two things are one more than the strict pantheist or the Soul of *The Palace of Art* will allow.

In rejecting pure pantheism, Tennyson also rejected its concomitant artistic theory, that all forms and genres are false, illusory limitations, meant to be shattered or collected and thereby captured in their totality. (Collection is the Soul's method of achieving artistic unity in her Palace, and in this she makes the mistake of believing that the number of forms in the universe is finite and that she will be able to gather them all.) Fittingly enough, the Soul's path back to health lies in her retreat to the "cottage in the vale."[18] She falls back on the setting of the pastoral idyll that had been the formal point of departure for Vergil's art:

> "Make me a cottage in the vale," she said,
>   "Where I may mourn and pray.
> Yet pull not down my palace towers, that are
>   So lightly, beautifully built:
> Perchance I may return with others there
>   When I have purged my guilt."   (291–296)

The Soul has learned the lesson that the young poet must also learn, especially if he is a young poet who hopes to embrace the whole of creation in his poetry and give a general description of the nexus of human psychology: the epical Palace of Art cannot be stormed in a single maneuver; it must be approached with humility, and the mode that best accommodates this humility, both for the Soul and the poet, is the idyll. The Soul's Palace, in the end, is not torn down, but exists as a goal to be reentered after purgation. Just so Tennyson hoped to approach the epic through the idyll.

Tennyson consciously chose for his early work a traditional poetic form encompassing a high degree of objectivity and distance. In selecting the idyll form, he sacrificed the immediacy of the Romantic poets to the manipulation of traditional forms, and to modern critics this has seemed an abandonment of visionary poetics. But the idyll form is sly, various, and above all, ambitious. By its very artificiality, by its dissociation of artist and poetic persona, it creates distance between the reader and the poetry. But behind this same artifice is a strongly held belief, the belief that dictated the creation of the idyll in the Greek world: poetry should not only feel the world, but know it simultaneously, even while the world is in the process of flux. Thus the idyll is an answer to Heraclitus' dilemma that we do not step twice into the same river: if, as the statement implies, the world is entirely a process or flow, where can we obtain a purchase from which to know it? Does one not rather have simply to move with the flow, knowing only the immediate sensation of existing in the flux? The idyll invariably describes this world of fluidity (and Tennyson was fond of writing about Heraclitus), but it does so in a way that makes the flow of emotions constituting the nexus of life knowable; it moves with, but at a distance from, the drama it describes, maintaining its objectivity and freedom even while it is immersed in the world of its subject. Tennyson did not pick the idyll for its ease, or out of a false sense of reverence for tradition, but for the very reason that the sinful Soul chooses the "cottage in the vale": because the way back to the Palace of Art, from which the young poet is driven by pride and inadequacy, lies through apprenticeship in the discipline of idyll.

FOUR
The English Idyls
and Other Poems

WITH THE PUBLICATION of the 1842 edition of his poems, Tennyson committed himself even more fully than in 1832 to the idyll form. The first eleven poems in the second volume were, in order,

> *The Epic*
> *Morte d'Arthur*
> *The Gardener's Daughter; or, The Pictures*
> *Dora*
> *Audley Court*
> *Walking to the Mail*
> *St. Simeon Stylites*
> *The Talking Oak*
> *Love and Duty*
> *Ulysses*
> *Locksley Hall*

In subsequent republications, Tennyson altered and added to this arrangement of poems, until in the 1884 edition of his collected works he arrived at the following order:

> *The Epic*
> *Morte d'Arthur*
> *The Gardener's Daughter; or, The Pictures*
> *Dora*
> *Audley Court*

Walking to the Mail
Edwin Morris; or, The Lake
St. Simeon Stylites   .
The Talking Oak
Love and Duty
The Golden Year
Ulysses
Tithonus
Locksley Hall

He had added, but not at random, three similar pieces that had not been published in 1842: *Tithonus*, in its revised form, which joined *Ulysses* (they had been written in 1833); *The Golden Year*, published in 1846; and *Edwin Morris*, published in 1851. From 1884 onward, these fourteen poems stood, in the same order, at the head of the division of his work that Tennyson designated "English Idyls and Other Poems."

Although Tennyson never specified exactly which poems he intended to include under the heading English Idyls, they have traditionally been regarded as those verses descriptive of English country life and history. *The Gardener's Daughter, Dora, Audley Court, Walking to the Mail, Edwin Morris, The Talking Oak, Love and Duty, The Golden Year, Locksley Hall*—these are clearly English Idyls. Yet in Tennyson's arrangement they are not grouped together but interspersed with poems like the *Morte d'Arthur* and *Ulysses* that are conceived on the model of classical idyll; hence the title "English Idyls and Other Poems," for at least in the series made up of the first fourteen works in this division of his verse, Tennyson is engaged in conscious manipulation of various idyll forms to achieve a unified effect.

The fourteen poems that comprise this series of idylls are given in three divisions. First, there are *The Epic* and the poem it introduces, *Morte d'Arthur*, which provide a preface to the twelve linked poems that follow. These twelve are in turn given in two sections. The first five poems, from *The Gardener's Daughter* through *Edwin Morris*, examine the various attitudes and emotions that can infect the pastoral world of idyll, and the remaining seven poems study how people respond to a world flawed in the

ways described by the first five idylls. This curious mixture
of epic themes and idyllic pictures is not so paradoxical as
it may at first seem. As he would do in *The Idylls of the
King*, Tennyson added poems to his collection of idylls till
he reached the epic number of twelve, and taken together
these twelve idylls form a quasi-epic on the psychology of
fulfillment.

In *The Epic*, the first of the two poems with epic ambitions prefacing the twelve linked idylls of this series, Tennyson discusses some of the problems about form that trouble
a modern poet:

> "You know," said Frank, "he burnt
> His epic, his King Arthur, some twelve books"—
> And then to me demanding why? "Oh sir,
> He thought that nothing new was said, or else
> Something so said 'twas nothing—that a truth
> Looks freshest in the fashion of the day:
> God knows: he has a mint of reasons: ask.
> It pleased *me* well enough." "Nay, nay," said Hall,
> "Why take the style of those heroic times?
> For nature brings not back the Mastodon,
> Nor we those times; and why should any man
> Remodel models? these twelve books of mine
> Were faint Homeric echoes, nothing-worth,
> Mere chaff and draff, much better burnt." "But I,"
> Said Francis, "picked the eleventh from this hearth
> And have it: keep a thing, its use will come."   (27–42)

In this introductory dialogue between the fictional poet
Hall and his friend Francis,[1] Tennyson touches on two of
the stimuli that in his conception of the tradition drive poets
to the idyll—the sense that everything has already been done
and the need, in spite of this, to go forward. Tradition, at
least for Francis, is not a thing from which we move con-
tinually farther away, but the circular movement of history:
"keep a thing, its use will come." Similarly, the poets of
Alexandria had returned to the literary traditions of the
Greek world and used them. With the publication of *Morte
d'Arthur*, Tennyson announced that he would do the same:
he would keep the old forms of epic and idyll and find a

modern application for them. *Morte d'Arthur* is both idyll and epic, and it is appropriate that Tennyson placed it at the beginning of this series of poems, since the idyll as epic is a fitting introduction to the twelve poems following it in "The English Idyls and Other Poems." *Morte d'Arthur* is not only an idyll in search of an epic (and in this it is related to the formal concerns of *The Palace of Art*); it is, of course, the quintessential "English Idyl," since its subject is Britain's archetypal monarch, Arthur. The spectacle of the King's and the kingdom's desolation in *Morte d'Arthur* provides a note of caution to be mixed with the pastoral landscapes of the English Idyls, and its epic structure alerts the reader to the possibility of structure among the twelve succeeding idylls.

The poems following the *Morte d'Arthur* begin, in *The Gardener's Daughter*, with a pastoral joy that is the polar opposite of Arthur's grim battlefield farewell, and they move forward with a plan that demonstrates the dissolution of this pastoral world, until, in *Locksley Hall*, they come full circle, confronting the reader with a modern version of the "barren land" of Lyonesse and a contemporary warrior who also goes to sea in defeat. These twelve poems can be treated as a series, united not only in being idylls of various sorts, but in several other ways. First, their focus is masculine: all the first-person narrators in the series are men; only in *Dora*, where attention is directed to the family, is the focus of the poem not male. Second, these poems share a similar landscape. And third, they discuss a single question (the same question posed in those later twelve interlocking poems, *The Idylls of the King*): is it possible, within the confines of the created world, to fulfill one's conscientious obligations to self and higher idealism while at the same time living a pragmatic and useful life in human society? More simply put, in the words of one of Tennyson's titles in this series, can one satisfy the demands of both love and duty? Tennyson investigates the question in these twelve idylls, beginning with portraits of the various bonds that unite people—romantic love, family ties, friendship, the larger nexus of society. Even as he is sketching out these basic relationships, he is also engaged in demonstrating what can go wrong with them. His first idyll in the series, *The Gardener's Daughter*, is a portrait of harmonious love, but the idylls following it examine successive conditions that threaten this ideal state. When he has depicted the major human relations in the first five idylls, he turns, in the last seven, to examine various attitudes that can be adopted in the face of the bewildering and often demoralizing emotions constituting the complex of bonds and emotions he has already described. The interaction of themes and attitudes among these twelve poems is mirrored by a corresponding manipulation of the varieties of idyll form, with the structure of each idyll substantiating and reinforcing its role in the series.

The Gardener's Daughter is Tennyson's portrait of the marriage of the creative spirit and the created world, of the satisfaction of the purely personal ambition of the heart as well as its desire to reach out to the world. It is, like the later *Coming of Arthur* in *The Idylls of the King*, an idyll of harmony, drawn in this case after the model of Theocritus, from whose seventh idyll Tennyson borrowed heavily in constructing the poem. He even approximates the name of one of Theocritus' characters, Eucritus, in calling one of his own characters Eustace. It was, of course, no accident that Tennyson borrowed his idyll of perfection from Theocritus' most utopian production. The curiosity is that Tennyson placed his paradisiacal idyll first in his series while Theocritus placed his last: for the Greek, the world built up to the perfect; for the Englishman, it declined from Eden. The same pattern was to obtain in *The Idylls of the King*.

In *The Gardener's Daughter*, the artist-narrator leaves the city for the day with his "brother-in-art," Eustace. Even their friendship partakes of the poem's overall harmony, for it is

> a friendship so complete
> Portioned in halves between us, that we grew
> The fable of the city where we dwelt. (4–6)

Eustace, who loves Juliet, maintains a friendly rivalry with the narrator, and showing him Juliet's portrait, asks, "When will *you* paint like this" (22), to which the narrator replies,

'Tis not your work, but Love's. Love, unperceived,
A more ideal Artist he than all,
Came, drew your pencil from you, made those eyes
Darker than darkest pansies, and that hair
More black than ashbuds in the front of March.   (24–28)

Juliet then tells the narrator that to find the inspiration of
love he is demanding for his art he should seek out the
gardener's daughter, which he does. He finds her in a landscape that will be common to the twelve idylls in this series:

Not wholly in the busy world, nor quite
Beyond it, blooms the garden that I love.
News from the humming city comes to it
In sound of funeral or of marriage bells;
And, sitting muffled in dark leaves, you hear
The windy clanging of the minster clock;
Although between it and the garden lies
A league of grass, washed by a slow broad stream,
That, stirred with languid pulses of the oar,
Waves all its lazy lilies, and creeps on,
Barge-laden, to three arches of a bridge
Crowned with the minster-towers.
                                    The fields between
Are dewy-fresh, browsed by deep-uddered kine,
And all about the large lime feathers low,
The lime a summer home of murmurous wings.   (33–47)

Here, as befits an idyll of harmony, the season is spring,
as it is at the opening of *The Idylls of the King*.[2] The
garden, like Camelot dancing in front of Gareth's eyes in
Gareth and Lynette, is "not wholly in the busy world, nor
quite / Beyond it." The city, from which the narrator has
come, can barely be discerned from the garden, which is
bathed in sun and shade; and nearby, the minster, the Gothic
church, commands the horizon.[3] A stream (very much like
the stream that encircles the Lady of Shalott) winds through
the garden area, and "lazy lilies" float on the tide. The
"murmurous wings" of bees lend music to the air.[4]

The only human, besides the narrator, who moves through
this landscape is the gardener's daughter. Her father is never
mentioned; indeed, from the moment she first appears, the

poem gives the impression that there are only two people
in the world, the lover and his beloved. When he first sees
her, she is tending the flowers in the garden of the country
house:

> I turned,
> And, ere a star can wink, beheld her there.

> For up the porch there grew an Eastern rose,
> That, flowering high, the last night's gale had caught,
> And blown across the walk. One arm aloft—
> Gowned in pure white, that fitted to the shape—
> Holding the bush, to fix it back, she stood,
> A single stream of all her soft brown hair
> Poured on one side: the shadow of the flowers
> Stole all the golden gloss, and wavering,
> Lovingly lower, trembled on her waist—
> Ah, happy shade—and still went wavering down,
> But, ere it touched a foot, that might have danced
> The greensward into greener circles, dipt
> And mixed with shadows of the common ground!
> But the full day dwelt on her brows, and sunned
> Her violet eyes, and all her Hebe bloom,
> And doubled his own warmth against her lips,
> And on the bounteous wave of such a breast
> As never pencil drew. Half light, half shade,
> She stood, a sight to make an old man young.   (120–140)

Tennyson said of this description that it "must be full and
rich," and indeed it is. Its richness stresses the identification
of the gardener's daughter with the natural world, so that
the artist, in wooing her, courts both the girl and nature
itself. She marries him, and the artist is doubly blest; he not
only has found a source of continued inspiration, but has
wedded it and possesses its love. His art and his passion are
indistinguishable.

At the end of the poem, the artist-narrator, now an old
man, tells a visitor the story of his courtship and marriage.
He addresses his guest:

> But this whole hour your eyes have been intent
> On that veiled picture, veiled, for what it holds
> May not be dwelt on by the common day.

> This prelude has prepared thee. Raise thy soul;
> Make thine heart ready with thine eyes: the time
> Is come to raise the veil.
>   Behold her there,
> As I beheld her ere she knew my heart,
> My first, last love; the idol of my youth,
> The darling of my manhood, and alas!
> Now the most blessed memory of mine age. (264–273)

Though his wife has died, she remains the "blessed memory" of his life in the world and the focal point of his artistry. Their love, which existed in time, has overcome time and now lives on in art. Indeed, the picture of the beloved, the unveiling of which closes the idyll, provides a perfect formal conclusion to the poem. This idyll is quite literally "framed"; inside the frame of the artist's narrative there is a word picture of the very person he unveils to the guest. The poem is a description of perfection through art, and it is itself artistically perfect.[5]

The Gardener's Daughter makes clear that nature cooperates to bring about the lovers' happiness, and in this it is an appropriate successor to the early *Miller's Daughter*. In the landscape the "birds have joyful thoughts," and they sing because

>   Were there nothing else
> For which to praise the heavens but only love,
> That only love were cause enough for praise. (102–104)

Here is the true Theocritean universe, knit together with invisible filaments of the love god, who conspires to bless the lives of mortals submitting to his sweet rule. Tennyson expresses this view again in the metaphor that the narrator employs to describe his emotions on first seeing his beloved:

>   vague desires, like fitful blasts of balm
> To one that travels quickly, made the air
> Of Life delicious, and all kinds of thoughts,
> That verged up on them, sweeter than the dream
> Dreamed by a happy man, when the dark East,
> Unseen, is brightening to his bridal morn.   (67–72)

The lover's bliss is made perfect by his willingness to indulge the natural flow of emotions and events; it is like a
happy dream, dictated by a joyous unconscious, one for
which the East, "unseen," prepares a waking finale more
exquisite than the dream itself.[6]

The modern reader will feel that this view of the possibility of human happiness glosses over a great deal of the
turmoil and heartbreak attendant upon love; indeed it does,
and purposely. The goal of this first idyll in the series of
twelve is to set up a perfect condition against which to contrast the various flawed states depicted in succeeding poems.
The Gardener's Daughter is remarkable for its isolated lovers, seemingly bound by no other restraints than those imposed by their own hearts. But in *Dora*, the idyll that immediately follows, in which Tennyson examines the family
and the fund of love that it implies, the course of love runs
less true. William and Dora are cousins, both living on
Allan's farm. Allan tells William, his son, that he wants him
to marry Dora, but William's response is truculent:

> William answered madly; bit his lips,
> And broke away. The more he looked at her
> The less he liked her.   (31–33)

Allan banishes William, who, "half in love, half spite" (37),
marries another girl, Mary. William has a son, then dies.
Through the abandoned Dora's exertions the outcast Mary
and her child are finally reconciled to Allan, who repents:

> the man was broken with remorse;
> And all his love came back a hundredfold;
> And for three hours he sobbed o'er William's child
> Thinking of William.   (161–164)

Tennyson built this idyll of country life with Old Testa-
ment simplicity in mind, and it is so simple that at times it
lapses into prose.[7] Its characters are deliberate stereotypes,
and its language is the overstatement of melodrama: "never
more darken my doors again," says Allan to his son. The
oversimplification on Tennyson's part is a purposely bald
statement of what can go wrong with the pretty universe

of *The Gardener's Daughter.* (The styles of the two poems are an almost violent contrast between lush Alexandrian diction and Hebraic leanness.) William's willfulness, his father's stubbornness, and the pride of both conspire to destroy the happiness of all concerned, and only the humility and patience of Dora can patch up the broken family ties.

In *Dora,* which is Tennyson's first statement in this series that love cannot be dictated as a social arrangement convenient for the family, he has chosen not a wealthy family but a simple farming household in order to make his point universally applicable. Several of the idylls that follow deal with the possibility of happiness within the boundaries of society, but all of them are extensions of the premise so simply presented in *Dora,* that the family, which is supposedly the outward sign of love's fulfillment, can paradoxically be an impediment to love.

The next poem, *Audley Court,* returns wholeheartedly to the Alexandrian style of idyll. It is modeled on the amoeban singing contests of Theocritus and Vergil, here modernized in a picnic scene between the narrator and his friend Francis Hale, "the farmer's son who lived across the bay" (74). Francis is probably made a farmer's son to provide continuity with *Dora,* while the narrator,

> having wherewithal,
> And in the fallow leisure of my life
> A rolling stone of here and everywhere   (76–78)

prepares the reader for the young men of *Edwin Morris* and *Locksley Hall.*[8] The subject of this idyll is still love, but the love of man for man, a theme that, though treated homoerotically in the classical models, Tennyson deals with in terms of straightforward friendship. Because he considered the bond of friendship one of the basic elements in the structure of human society, he placed this idyll of friendship immediately after his idylls of romantic love and family life in this series of twelve poems designed to demonstrate the fundamental relations of civilization and the forces that attack them. Francis and the narrator have their picnic and singing match on the lawns beside the gardener's lodge of Audley Court, which the Audley family has recently lost as the result of their financial collapse. The poem is set in 1837, and the Audley's bankruptcy may be the result of the unstable economic conditions of the 1830s. More important, however, the poem treats the universal endurance of friendship against a background of social flux: "who would rent the hall" (30) is one of the friends' topics, and later the narrator mentions that he has bought one of Sir Robert's books—presumably in the sale liquidating the estate—when they "came to the hammer here in March" (59). The ruined estate adds still more elements to the landscape of the Tennysonian idyll, which had purposely been portrayed in *The Gardener's Daughter* as primarily natural. Here the class structure and the larger social world of historical flux make their appearance, though these forces do not as yet impinge on the speaking characters of the poem, whose friendship crosses class lines and endures despite hard times. In *Audley Court* the destructive power of social forces is only hinted at, but the themes that have been unobtrusively introduced will be more fully developed in the idylls that follow.

The fallen house appears again in *Walking to the Mail*. The situation of the poem continues the friendship theme of *Audley Court* in a related structure much like the singing contest of classical idyll, but now against a new, more disturbing backdrop. Two friends are walking down to meet the mail coach. The mail delivery is indicative of larger relations among mankind than those of family and friends already explored in these idylls, and against the background of this larger social nexus the speakers, James and John, hold their conversation. They discuss Sir Edward Head, lord of the local estate, who has abandoned his land and whose house "is to be sold" (11). This, of course, is the situation of *Audley Court*, now more fully developed. Sir Edward has fled to escape both the political change mentioned in *Audley Court* and a bad marriage—the two problems are related. He is said to have "a morbid devil in his blood / That veiled the world with jaundice" (13–14). James feels Sir Edward's lapse from felicity has been occasioned by his wife:

> the blossom fades, and they that loved
> At first like dove and dove were cat and dog.

She was the daughter of a cottager,
Out of her sphere. What betwixt shame and pride,
New things and old, himself and her, she soured
To what she is: a nature never kind!   (49-54)

The idyll develops the class consciousness that was latent
in the friendship of the narrator and Francis in *Audley
Court*. Sir Edward's marriage out of his class has resulted in
unhappiness, whereas in the better known *Locksley Hall*
and *Maud*, the narrators profess that the *failure* to marry
across class lines for love is the root of unhappiness—but then
these poems are all idylls and portray their speakers' emotions, not Tennyson's. In her unaccustomed position, Sir
Edward's wife has "soured"; the combined shock to breed-
ing and manners has destroyed his life, and the hall stands
vacant.

An analogous shock for Sir Edward was the political situation of the 1830s. (The poem was written at the start of the
Chartist agitations.)

I was once near him, when his bailiff brought
A Chartist pike. You should have seen him wince
As from a venomous thing: he thought himself
A mark for all, and shuddered, lest a cry
Should break his sleep by night, and his nice eyes
Should see the raw mechanic's bloody thumbs
Sweat on his blazoned chairs; but, sir, you know
That these two parties shall divide the world—
Of those that want and those that have: and still
The same old sore breaks out from age to age
With much the same result.   (61-72)

The marriage of rich and poor, mimicked by Sir Edward's
alliance with the cottager's daughter, has also fallen apart and
the speaker views the dissolution of such unions as inevitable:
"The same old sore breaks out from age to age." To explain
why this sort of union must fail—we have now come a long
way from the perfect union of art and beauty in *The
Gardener's Daughter*, which was also a marriage of the
leisured and the lower classes—Tennyson has one of his
speakers tell a half-comic, half-serious anecdote:

Now I myself,
A Tory to the quick, was as a boy
Destructive, when I had not what I would.
I was at school—a college in the South:
There lived a flayflint near; we stole his fruit,
His hens, his eggs; but there was law for *us*;
We paid in person. He had a sow, sir. She,
With meditative grunts of much content,
Lay great with pig, wallowing in sun and mud.
By night we dragged her to the college tower
From her warm bed, and up the corkscrew stair
With hand and rope we haled the groaning sow,
And on the leads we kept her till she pigged.
Large range of prospect had the mother sow,
And but for daily loss of one she loved
As one by one we took them—but for this—
As never sow was higher in this world—
Might have been happy: but what lot is pure?
We took them all, till she was left alone
Upon her tower, the Niobe of swine,
And so returned unfarrowed to her sty.   (72–92)

In this pastoral episode, the speaker, James, whose view
may be taken as a conservative statement on the subject—
he is "a Tory to the quick"—portrays, in a story reminiscent
of Augustine's demonstration of original sin from his boy-
hood theft of pears, the willfulness of childhood as a baleful
but permanent constituent of the psychological universe. Its
presence in human affairs makes all relations, in politics or
love, doubtful, as the other speaker points out:

What know we of the secret of a man?
His nerves were wrong. What ails us, who are sound,
That we should mimic this raw fool of the world,
Which charts us all in its coarse blacks or whites,
As ruthless as a baby with a worm,
As cruel as a schoolboy ere he grows
To Pity—more from ignorance than will.   (94–100)

The speaker, John, does not go so far as Augustine—he attributes the schoolboy cruelty of the world to cosmic
ignorance, not infected will, but the result is the same in

either case: a world in which the perfection of *The Gardener's Daughter* has given way to the destructive behavior exhibited here and in *Dora*, which finally corrupts the whole social fabric, as it had, by implication, in the Chartist movement.

Nor is it possible to escape from this poison in human affairs. Sir Edward Head has tried to flee, but another anecdote is added to demonstrate the vanity of his attempt. Sir Edward's tenant, Jocky Dawes, similarly tried to run away from a ghost that haunted his house. When he had packed up and was riding away from the house, he found the meddlesome spirit had accompanied him: "Oh well," said Jocky, "you flitting with us too— / Jack, turn the horses' heads and home again" (37–38). The gist of the idyll as a whole is that one can neither prevent the "morbid devil" in the blood nor flee from it. It is a grim idyll, saved from bitterness only by its light tone, and it brings to the continuing study of the possibility of human happiness a new complexity.

The next poem, *Edwin Morris*, not only fills out the first division of five idylls in this series of twelve but also includes elements of the tradition of idyll and of all its predecessors in Tennyson's series. The poem is both a love lament in the style of Theocritus' *Cyclops* and amoeban verse in the conversational give-and-take of the singing-match idyll. Like *The Gardener's Daughter*, it is narrated by an artist who looks back on a love affair, but his romance has ended unhappily. As in *Audley Court*, the narrator has a close friend (unlike the more sanguine *Audley Court* the poem shows us the end of his friendship), Edwin Morris himself, who is thirty years older than the speaker and whose own romance was perfect like that in *The Gardener's Daughter*. Morris describes it in terms reminiscent of the earlier poem: "My love for Nature, and my love for her, / Of different ages, like twin-sisters grew" (32–33). The narrator hopes to copy Morris in his own love of Letty Hill, the daughter of a nouveau-riche industrial family. These arrivistes, now ensconced in the local estate, are the answer to the question persisting throughout the two previous idylls as to who shall take over the manor:

> new-comers in the ancient hold,
> New-comers from the Mersey, millionaires,
> Here lived the Hills. (9–11)

He succeeds with the girl, but not with her family.[9] Letty pledges her love and meets him one morning in the garden of the Hills' new manor. Whereas Tennyson had made the garden of *The Gardener's Daughter* "that Eden where she dwelt" (187), he describes Letty in her garden as Milton portrayed Eve in Paradise: "she moved / Like Proserpine in Enna, gathering flowers" (111–112). As Proserpine to Dis and Eve to Satan, Letty succumbs, here to her family's concepts of social obligation, and love is thwarted by a mercenary ideal of duty:

> in one month
> They wedded her to sixty thousand pounds,
> To lands in Kent and messuages in York,
> And slight Sir Robert with his watery smile
> And educated whisker. (125–128)

After this, the garden world only exists as a memory for the narrator, who lives out his life "in the dust and drouth of London life" (143), his pastoral aspirations to romance crushed. Nature is no longer a medium for conciliation and mating, as it has been in *The Gardener's Daughter* and for Edwin Morris, the speaker's friend; it becomes instead problematic and ambiguous:

> She moves among my visions of the lake,
> While the prime swallow dips his wing, or then
> While the gold-lily blows, and overhead
> The light cloud smoulders on the summer crag.
> (144–147)

The cloud "smoulders" on the crag: there are hidden fires in nature that threaten what now appears to be the very tenuous possibility of human happiness. (They may manifest themselves in man's social relations, as here; or in his willfulness, as in *Walking to the Mail;* or in his pride, as in *Dora*). The first five poems in the series have now come full circle from the blissful "picture" of *The Gardener's Daughter*.

The seven idylls followings *Edwin Morris* accept the

premise that the world in which mankind seeks its fulfillment is, at least for the present, flawed, and they examine
the different attitudes possible for men to adopt in the
face of this reality. And these poems really do examine men:
with the exception of *Dora* all the idylls are told of or by
males who seem, in the most general terms, to represent the
interior human gradually emerging from his preoccupation
with self and reaching out toward the created world at large,
usually represented by the beloved, even though this world
is flawed in the ways described by the earlier idylls.

The most violent reaction to such a world, of course,
would be to withdraw from it entirely, and this is precisely
the attitude Tennyson examines in *St. Simeon Stylites*. The
anchorite, who spent thirty years suspended between heaven
and earth on a pillar (his "celestial life," Edward Gibbon
called it)[10] is roundly execrated by Tennyson in this satiric
monologue written in the style of Horace and Juvenal. Of
all Tennyson's poems it comes closest in style to Browning:

> I die here
> Today, and whole years long, a life of death.
> Bear witness, if I could have found a way
> (And heedfully I sifted all my thought)
> More slowly-painful to subdue this home
> Of sin, my flesh, which I despise and hate.   (53–58)

His flight from the world (not unlike Sir Edward's in *Walking to the Mail*) is attended by a "morbid devil." In this
case pride torments the saint. His vulgar martyrdom is seen
as a vicious form of self-indulgence:

> Good people, you do ill to kneel to me.
> What is it I can have done to merit this?
> I am a sinner viler than you all.
> It may be I have wrought some miracles
> And cured some halt and maimed, but what of that?
> (131–135)

Indeed, the whole monologue is loosely based on Chaucer's
Pardoner's prologue, and Tennyson's Simeon is if anything
more despicable, more outcast from the human community,
than Chaucer's hypocrite. As Gibbon said of Simeon, "This
voluntary martyrdom must have gradually destroyed the

sensibility both of the mind and body; nor can it be presumed that the fanatics who torment themselves are susceptible of any lively affection for the rest of mankind." Tennyson places his tawdry saint here among his idylls as an exemplum, very much along Chaucerian lines, of one disastrous response men make to the initial disillusionment they suffer with the world.[11]

The Talking Oak is a fitting companion piece for *St. Simeon Stylites* because it presents the complementary perspective. Whereas *St. Simeon Stylites* is an invective satire in the Roman tradition, *The Talking Oak* is a gentle comedy that reminds one of *As You Like It*.[12] Once again, the English landscape made familiar by the first idylls is employed, and the idyll takes the form of a whimsical dialogue between the familiar swain and the aged oak on the estate of his beloved. *St. Simeon Stylites* portrayed a man who had disavowed any contact with the created world, who literally refused to partake of earth and lived in the air. In *The Talking Oak*, the speaker, the oak itself, is entirely earthbound, but by mediating between the lover and his beloved it demonstrates that nature is cooperative with man in his quest for fulfillment in the world. Not that the created world is wholly benign in this idyll. The oak itself introduces an historical note into the poem by mentioning its past: it has lived long enough to remember the estate as a monastery (perhaps a memory meant to connect this poem with the monastic Simeon), the reign of Henry VIII, the Revolution, and the death of Cromwell. As Tennyson noted, the oak is an "old Tory," and it strictly disapproves of Cromwell and his Roundheads, first as promoters of "puritanic stays" (60) and then as rehearsers of a "surly hymn" (300). The history the oak has witnessed has included much restraint of natural impulse (the abbey, the Puritans), but history itself is a progress toward fulfillment; hence the tree's concern for an acorn fallen from its boughs. And time produces people and events that are better and better, so that the beloved of the poem, Olivia, is the most beautiful in a series of beautiful girls the tree has seen:

> I swear (and else may insects prick
> Each leaf into a gall)

> This girl, for whom your heart is sick,
> Is three times worth them all. (69–72)

Here the belief in time, as a dispensation in which the now
far-off garden of *The Gardener's Daughter* can be recap-
tured, gradually begins to dominate this series of idylls.

The goodness of time is reaffirmed in *Love and Duty*, the
poem that follows *The Talking Oak*. In it the central themes
of all the idylls in the series are presented: the struggle for
fulfillment in the world, which is the impulse of love
(thwarted in this poem because the lovers' sense of duty to
self and society dictates a separation); the need to reconcile
love with the demands of some interior, conscientious
monitor, here called duty; and the question as to how, if
at all, the conflict between these two principles can be resolved in time.[13] The earlier idylls in this series traced the
forces that blighted the possibility of human happiness and
began to discuss possible attitudes to take toward a less-
than-perfect world. *Love and Duty* presents an alternative
to *St. Simeon Stylites* and also to *The Talking Oak*, in which
time brought happiness. Here time appears to bring separation and misery, and an act of faith is required before the
speaker's situation can make any sense to him:

> Wait, and Love himself will bring
> The drooping flower of knowledge changed to fruit
> Of wisdom. Wait: my faith is large in Time,
> And that which shapes it to some perfect end. (23–26)

Time brings its setbacks, as it brought its Cromwells in *The
Talking Oak*, but finally time conspires with the good:

> The slow sweet hours that bring us all things good,
> The slow sad hours that bring us all things ill,
> And all good things from evil. (56–58)

The human will is capable in any eventuality:

> Live—yet live—
> Shall sharpest pathos blight us, knowing all
> Life needs for life is possible to will—
> Live happy; tend thy flowers. (81–84)

In the end the poem shows the beloved, as in *The Gardener's Daughter*, happy among her flowers. It is no longer the spontaneous, unchecked joy of that poem, however, but a happiness won by disappointment turned to fortitude through faith in love's eventual triumph in time. Time will, it is hoped, bring a reconciliation of the now conflicting demands of love and duty.

The Golden Year takes up the problem of time again, in ways that consciously echo Vergil's fourth eclogue; the question will be kept before the reader through *Locksley Hall*, the final idyll in this series. In *The Golden Year* the faith of *Love and Duty* is espoused by one speaker, Leonard, and rebutted by another, James. (The poem takes the form of the pastoral singing match between friendly swains in modern dress, as in *Audley Court*.) Leonard maintains that a "golden year," something like that in Vergil's fourth eclogue, is imminent:

> We sleep and wake and sleep, but all things move;
> The Sun flies forward to his brother Sun;
> The dark Earth follows wheeled in her ellipse;
> And human things returning on themselves
> Move onward, leading up the golden year.   (22–26)

Like Vergil's golden age, Leonard's is not an entirely new phenomenon toward which the creation moves, but an ancient state of original perfection to which it returns: "magnus ab integro saeclorum nascitur ordo" (4.5) ("the great order of the ages is born anew"), Vergil has it in the *Eclogues*. Likewise Leonard's "human things" return on themselves. This is at once a consoling and a limiting hope, for if time brings the spectacle of repetition, then human endeavor is finite and exhaustible. Believing this, Leonard applies the doctrine to poetry itself and finds the forms of artistic expression depleted:

> I was born too late: the fair new forms,
> That float about the threshold of an age,
> Like truths of Science waiting to be caught—
> Catch me who can, and make the catcher crowned—
> Are taken by the forelock.   (15–19)

Like the planets in their cycle, Leonard's forms must repeat their courses, and what is true of Leonard's poems would seem to be true of Tennyson's—they come full circle and duplicate the classical models. But Leonard's is not by any means the definitive notion of time in this poem, nor is his the definitive poetry. Tennyson's second speaker, James, refutes Leonard:

> What stuff is this!
> Old writers pushed the happy season back,—
> The more fools they,—we forward: dreamers both.
>
> (71–73)

James is cast in the role of Carlyle in this idyll and argues for a golden year present or not present to each individual according as he fulfills his allotted tasks in this world: "unto him who works, and feels he works, / This same grand year is ever at the doors" (72–73). The notion of doing one's work and finding happiness in the commitment to this personal duty is included as a modification of Leonard's more romantic concept of time, and it also modifies the ancilliary concept of forms; for if work is all, it does not matter whether poetic forms repeat themselves in time as long as the artist fulfills himself in the work at hand. James's view of time, like Carlyle's, is austere, perhaps even ominous: as he speaks, the sounds of blasting in a nearby quarry "buffet round the hills" (76). The devotion to work that James advocates can become an obsessive, explosive crusade of self-indulgence, and the quarrymen's blasts suggest that it may be the apocalypse rather than the golden age that is impending.

These opposing notions of how time should best be understood in order to achieve the fulfillment that eluded speakers in the earlier idylls are further discussed and modified in the next two poems, *Ulysses* and *Tithonus*.

Ulysses echoes *The Golden Year* in his dictum, "To strive, to seek, to find, and not to yield" (70). For Ulysses, the garden state of human realization is not obtained externally, for its "margin fades / For ever and for ever when I move" (20–21), but through constant activity in the satisfaction of an internal compulsion, in this case, toward knowledge:

> but every hour is saved
> From that eternal silence, something more,
> A bringer of new things; and vile it were
> For some three suns to store and hoard myself,
> And this gray spirit yearning in desire
> To follow knowledge like a sinking star,
> Beyond the utmost bound of human thought.   (27–32)

No more than James does Ulysses believe in time as a progress toward the ideal; it is rather a moment of activity in the "eternal silence" that is to be exploited to the full. The latent self-indulgence of James's Carlylian philosophy of work is demonstrated in its most heroic manner in the figure of Ulysses. His total commitment to the principle of action leads him to discard several of the components that elsewhere in these idylls are considered necessary elements of the good life. Beloved, family, society—in short, the network of human relations examined by Tennyson in this series of poems—Ulysses willingly surrenders. Penelope, who in Homer had been the goal of his odyssey, is now reduced to "an aged wife" (3). So much for romance. Family and social bonds are as easily dismissed:

> This is my son, mine own Telemachus,
> To whom I leave the sceptre and the isle—
> Well-loved of me, discerning to fulfill
> This labor, by slow prudence to make mild
> A rugged people, and through soft degrees
> Subdue them to the useful and the good.
> Most blameless is he, centered in the sphere
> Of common duties, decent not to fail
> In offices of tenderness, and pay
> Meet adoration to my household gods,
> When I am gone. He works his work, I mine. (33–43)

Ulysses, who assumes the opposite position from St. Simeon's in virtually all things—Ulysses believes "death closes all" (51), while Simeon thinks his glory will only begin with death—finally arrives at the same position as the saint: he is alone in the face of the whole world. Like Simeon, he has found fulfillment in a commitment to a basically self-centered concept of duty, and he disavows the other great principle that animates these idylls—love.

The familiar landscape of earlier idylls recurs in the scene framing Ulysses' departure:

> The lights begin to twinkle from the rocks:
> The long day wanes: the slow moon climbs: the deep
> Moans round with many voices. (54–56)

When the same scene was portrayed in *Audley Court*, it embraced the friendship of Francis Hale and the narrator:

> ere the night we rose
> And sauntered home beneath the moon, that, just
> In crescent, dimly rained about the leaf
> Twilights of airy silver, till we reached
> The limits of the hills; and as we sank
> From rock to rock upon the glooming quay,
> The town was hushed beneath us: lower down
> The bay was oily calm; the harbour-buoy,
> Sole star of phosphorescence in the calm,
> With one green sparkle ever and anon
> Dipt by itself, and we were glad at heart. (78–88)

In *Audley Court* the twilight sea was a tranquil reflection of the amity between the two friends. For Ulysses, who has no such friendship, there is no love to hold him to the land, and he strikes out across the ocean. When Tennyson used the same landscape at the end of *Love and Duty* (but in a sunrise rather than a sunset, to betoken the hope of that poem), it embodied the faith of the poem's narrator in the eventual justice of love:

> the first low matin-chirp hath grown
> Full quire, and morning driven her plow of pearl
> Far furrowing into light the moulded rack,
> Beyond the fair green field and eastern sea. (95–98)

But in *Ulysses* all human rapport is sacrificed to self and will, the besetting human defect examined in *Walking to the Mail*. James's work philosophy in *The Golden Year* is shown to be only partially satisfying, for it ignores the whole aspect of happiness that is embraced, not by self-fulfillment, but by shedding self to make room for the presence and comfort of others.

Tithonus has long been treated as a "pendant" to *Ulysses*.[14] It not only complements that poem but fits into the development of the other idylls as well, for Tithonus' curse is to live forever in the garden state of *The Gardener's Daughter*, to endure the golden year perpetually. The happy romances of these twelve idylls—those of *The Gardener's Daughter*, and *Edwin Morris*—are explicitly the recollections of older men recalling their youth, in which the beloved has died and the lover maintains her memory as an inspiration. Everywhere in these poems there is faith in the justice of time. For Tithonus, however, the justice of time is not a dispensation but a punishment:

> thy strong Hours indignant worked their wills,
> And beat me down and marred and wasted me,
> And though they could not end me, left me maimed
> To dwell in presence of immortal youth,
> Immortal age beside immortal youth,
> And all I was, in ashes. (18–23)

The indignant Hours are as much capable of punishing what they consider unworthy as they are of leading in the golden year. But what exactly is Tithonus' unworthiness? Not simply that he asked to live forever, but that he gave up his whole being to his love, which provoked him to make his request. Indeed, most of the poem is given over to descriptions of his love. Tithonus has succumbed to love so completely that he has laid aside his duty as a man:

> take back thy gift:
> Why should a man desire in any way
> To vary from the kindly race of men,
> Or pass beyond the goal of ordinance
> Where all should pause, as is most meet for all? (28–31)

The human duty is here encompassed in the word "ordinance," implying submission of self to the larger forces of nature and time. Ulysses made this submission a crusade; the narrator of *Love and Duty*, an act of faith; but Tithonus in his love for Aurora has repudiated it entirely. In *The Gardener's Daughter*, the idyll in this series that comes closest to describing harmony between man and nature, the beloved died and the lovers were separated by time, the eventuality that Tithonus dreads. But for Tennyson, Tithonus' alternative to death is the quintessential horror: to live with oneself for ever. And in fact, the perfection of *The Gardener's Daughter* depends upon the genial acceptance of the forces which Tithonus hoped to escape. By embracing only love and avoiding the human duty toward time and nature, Tithonus has rendered himself as selfish and lonely as Ulysses, though by embracing an opposite principle.

Locksley Hall is the final idyll in the series of twelve beginning with *The Gardener's Daughter*. It is not, as one might suspect, a triumphant return to the garden of the first poem in the series. It is rather a compilation of the various emotional states and attitudes of the eleven preceding idylls put in the mouth of a speaker who "represents young life, its good side, its deficiencies, and its yearnings."[15] But then, Vergil had ended his *Eclogues* with the death of Gallus: far from demanding a happy ending, the tradition in which Tennyson was working, as well as Tennyson's own disposition, allowed for a conclusion on a disturbing note.

The landscape of *Locksley Hall* is the familiar countryside, dominated as usual by the hall, and the situation of the idyll is the equally familiar romance of the girl in the hall, in this case Amy, the young narrator's cousin. As in *Edwin Morris*, the girl forsakes the narrator for a marriage of social duty. "Thou art mated with a clown," cries the narrator: "his eyes are heavy: think not they are glazed with wine. / Go to him: it is thy duty: kiss him: take his hand in thine" (51–52). As in previous idylls, the speaker believes the social nexus is an unnatural restraint on the free commerce of love:

Cursed be the social wants that sin against the strength of
    youth!
Cursed be the social lies that warp us from the living truth!

Cursed be the sickly forms that err from honest Nature's rule!
Cursed be the gold that gilds the straitened forehead of the
    fool!   (59–62)

The narrator here, as in *Edwin Morris,* finds the memory of his blighted romance bitter: "this is truth the poet sings, / That a sorrow's crown of sorrow is remembering happier things" (74–76). Here he repeats Dante's line in the *Inferno,*

> Nessun maggior dolore
> che ricordarsi del tempo felice
> nella miseria. (5.121–123)

In *Ulysses* there was constant irony in the knowledge that Tennyson's source was Dante's hell-bound adventurer, and in *Locksley Hall* Tennyson made the speaker echo the sentiments of Dante's fallen Francesca, trapped forever in the circle of the incontinent. Like Francesca's sin, the present narrator's emotions and rhetoric are self-indulgent; he possesses none of the resignation in the face of reality expressed in *Love and Duty.* Instead, he adopts a willful, Ulysses-like posture mixed with a portion of Leonard's idealism in *The Golden Year:*

> Yet I doubt not through the ages one increasing purpose runs,
> And the thoughts of men are widening with the process of
> the suns.
>
> What is that to him that reaps not harvest of his youthful joys,
> Though the deep heart of existence beat for ever like a boy's?
>
> Knowledge comes, but wisdom lingers, and I linger on the
> shore,
> And the individual withers, and the world is more and more.
>
> Knowledge comes, but wisdom lingers, and he bears a laden
> breast,
> Full of sad experience, moving toward the stillness of his rest.
> (137–144)

The attitudes of Ulysses, who also fears to linger on the beach while "the world is more and more," are here embodied in a thoroughly contemporary situation, and Ulysses' quest for knowledge becomes in this speaker a foretaste of Conrad's Kurtz:

> Ah, for some retreat
> Deep in younger shining Orient, where my life began to beat;
>
> . . . . .

There methinks would be enjoyment more than in this march
    of mind,
In the steamship, in the railway, in the thoughts that shake
    mankind.

There the passions cramped no longer shall have scope and
    breathing space;
I will take some savage woman, she shall rear my dusky race.
                  (153–154; 165–168)

For the young narrator, the new age is a blend of Leonard's
Vergilian *novum ordo saeclorum* and Carlylian vision—a
return to paradise won by hard work in the contemporary
marketplace. If the world does not provide an equal con-
summation of love and duty, the narrator will work to push
it forward to the time when it must do so: "Not in vain the
distance beacons. Forward, forward let us range, / Let the
great world spin for ever down the ringing grooves of
change" (181–182). It is not for this speaker to be a "gray
spirit yearning in desire"; he will strike out on the sea like
Ulysses and let Tithonus' decaying woods (the language of
this section echoes *Ulysses* and *Tithonus* closely) claim
what he considers the corrupt world of Locksley Hall:

       a long farewell to Locksley Hall!
Now for me the woods may wither, now for me the roof-tree
    fall.

Comes a vapour from the margin, blackening over heath and
    holt,
Cramming all the blast before it, in its breast a thunderbolt.

Let it fall on Locksley Hall, with rain or hail, or fire or snow;
For the mighty wind arises, roaring seaward, and I go.
                  (189–195)

And so the manor house, prominent throughout this series
of twelve idylls, is at its conclusion placed under a curse. It
is certainly a dramatic finale, though it does not, like *Love
and Duty*, represent Tennyson's own solution to the dilemma of time, love, and duty presented throughout the
idylls. It is, rather, a dramatic statement that amalgamates
the several strands of thought running through the idylls
and brings them to a resounding if imperfect conclusion in

the aspirations of a young man. But then, these idylls are not polemical: their speakers may indulge in polemics, but not the idylls themselves. They are descriptive, and *Locksley Hall* is, of this series, the fullest description of the emotional filaments that compound the vexed question of human happiness. With *Locksley Hall*, we have come from the garden in the first of these idylls, "not wholly in the busy world, nor quite / Beyond it," to the portrait of a man who rejects the garden world of the hall entirely and chooses to live only "in the busy world" of the modern era. Tennyson could not have approved of this choice—his arrangement of the poems put the young narrator of *Locksley Hall* at the ruined end of a spectrum beginning with the Eden of *The Gardener's Daughter*—but he may have believed it represented the reality of man's struggle to accommodate the warring forces of love and duty.

This series of twelve poems, then, continues Tennyson's several interests in the idyll form. It presents various emotional states in a way that blends the idyll's traditional penchant for allegory with the depiction of contemporary sensibility. The shabby-genteel swains of these poems move about in the English countryside adjoining the manor and not in the Sicilian meadows, but the poems continue the Theocritean tradition of representing in their songs isolated psychological conditions, so that they become partially allegorical. Each idyll has a narrow focus developed by one of the idyll's several formats, such as the framed story, the monologue, the singing contest, or the love lament, and each format is appropriate to the theme of its idyll. Hence *The Gardener's Daughter*, which is a painter's discourse on love, the most fundamental subject of idyll, is rendered in the most painterly form of idyll, the framed discourse, a device that has led many to believe the term idyll must mean "little picture." Tennyson seems consciously to be playing with this possible meaning of *eidyllion* in *The Gardener's Daughter*, but he is no more restricted by this one format than was Theocritus or Vergil, and he presents subsequent idylls in formats that both exploit the full range of the tradition on which he was drawing and reinforce his continuing argument. Thus *Walking to the Mail* and *Audley Court*, which are about friendship and social ties, are couched in the give-

and-take of the singing-contest idyll, a format common to the collection of both Theocritus and Vergil, while a monologue like *St. Simeon Stylites* draws on the idyll's roots in mime and on Roman satire in order to develop a format that will not only have the properties of idyllic monologue but moral bite as well.

These idylls manipulate the traditional formats of idyll and continue the psychological structuring typical of the form. Each separate idyll partakes of a larger, psychological pattern. The succession of idylls does not build to a climax, nor does it have a plot as normally conceived. What it does attempt, however, is to cover all the possible mental attitudes toward its chosen subject and to present these attitudes roundly and fully to the reader. Within this presentation there are links and patterns, as in the gradual broadening of the scope of the series from lovers to families to friends to society at large, and the reader is not so much invited to take sides as to enjoy the human spectacle in all its facets. Here, as Tennyson suggested in the *Ode to Memory*, the aim of poetry is to represent what is universal by depicting "all forms/Of the many-sided mind." With these poems, Tennyson achieved complete control of the idyll, as Vergil had in the *Eclogues*, and like his predecessor, he was then prepared to push beyond the form.

But while he teased the idyll form beyond its traditional bounds, Tennyson never relinquished his interest in the forms of idyll as he had perfected them back in 1842. Of his later "classical" idylls written after the model of *Ulysses* or *St. Simeon Stylites*, *Lucretius* (1868) is probably the most famous. The "domestic" idyll he continued in *Enoch Arden* (1864), in which the Theocritean poem of country life is given not only the rich verbal coloring of Alexandrian poetry but the concrete plot and character development of the nineteenth-century novel. Indeed, *Enoch Arden* is an excellent example of Tennyson's idyll pushing out to larger and larger proportions and engulfing various other genres in the process.

Yet it was not only the single idyll that fascinated Tennyson, but also the possibility of relating various idylls to one another in a series. Such a study in juxtaposition would eventually lead to the serial structuring of *In Memoriam* and *The Idylls of the King*. Even in the last poems he published, "*The Death of Oenone*," Tennyson was still experimenting with idyll and its arrangement. This volume of 1892, the year of his death, begins with *The Death of Oenone*, in which the mournful heroine of Tennyson's earlier *Oenone* is transformed into a hardhearted and unforgiving wife to a defeated Paris, who kills himself in despair. In pagan fashion (a fashion Akbar will denounce two poems later) Oenone joins her dead husband on the funeral pyre, her repentence coming late and destructively. *The Death of Oenone*, taken from the classical sources, is immediately followed in this volume by *St. Telemachus*, an idyll of the Christian era, in which death caused by narrow and uncomprehending human passion is again the subject: Telemachus dies in the Colosseum, a martyr to the Roman mob's thirst for human blood. This series of idylls is continued in *Akbar's Dream*, which follows in the proper chronological order after the classical and early Christian idylls, and the philosophy of the sixteenth-century Mogul ruler also follows the development of Tennyson's theme, for he advocates a quasi-pantheistic vision that transcends the crippling passions of humankind and makes common cause of the best elements of the pagan and monotheistic philosophies animating the two previous idylls in the series. The cultural progression of the idylls is clear—from blind passion in *The Death of Oenone* through struggling humanity in *St. Telemachus* to triumphant spiritual order in the discipline of higher truth accomplished in *Akbar's Dream*. The progress of these last Tennysonian idylls may also mirror the growth of the poet's mind and encapsulate his wide and inclusive use of tradition. Certainly it demonstrates that his interest in idyll and the relation of one idyll to another within a series were preoccupations that endured until his death.

FIVE
The Fuller Minstrel

THE IDYLL contains within it elements of most other poetic genres, and it manipulates these elements to its own ends. The writer of idylls is by definition a playful artificer; his craft is exercised in the detached, objective depiction of a world seen entirely as an aesthetic arrangement of often disparate components. In this commitment to artistry, the idyll is, however, irresolute. Subtle and sinuous as the links between various idylls in a collection may be, the form cannot in its native state pretend to the *gravitas* of the epic or the drama. The idyll's reliance upon objective studies of isolated mental states keeps it from asserting any larger, more fully proclaimed vision of life; and its essential playfulness, which encourages the reader to treat it as an aspect of the comic, also allows it to be dismissed as incapable of the serious vision associated with larger forms. The great poets have traditionally sought to escape the limitations of the idyll even as they used it; hence Vergil sang his *paulo maiora* in the *Eclogues* and Tennyson prefaced his most polished collection of idylls with *The Epic* and *Morte d'Arthur*.

The idyll has either to grow or to die. A poetic career that begins and ends in the idyll will always seem stunted, for the idyll form requires the poet to grow in his use of form. The idyll longs for the scope of its elder brother, epic, and envies Homeric grandeur. Both Vergil and Milton carried their training in idyll through to a larger conclusion, and Tennyson, having completed his apprenticeship in the form with the publication of the 1842 volumes, set about expanding the borders of his idyll in order to reach a poetry that might reflect the unity and seriousness of his larger vision.

For Vergil, the approach to the *Aeneid*, after he had completed the *Eclogues*, lay through the *Georgics*; for Milton, *Paradise Lost* was reached through *Lycidas* and *Comus*. If the way to epic has included Hesiodic farming manuals, elegy, and drama, the term Tennyson applied to his own progress may be accepted as an accurate description of the poetic journey toward the forms of larger vision—"the strange diagonal." His journey led to *In Memoriam*, but it began with *The Princess* (1847), which has often been called a sort of idyll (an "idyll protracted" was Eliot's term for it), for it does indeed preserve many of the devices of the idyll genre, even as it moves away from the form.[1]

The Princess: A Medley

Most obviously, *The Princess* is idyllic in its playfulness, for the comic mode of the poem is but an extension of the basic manipulative sportfulness of the early idylls. The conceit of a "medley," which gives the poem its subtitle, is only a less oblique notice of the process, already apparent in Tennyson's early career, of linking the various components of idylls to create a unified structure. This process, of course, is extended in *The Princess*. The epic tendency inherent in the idyll is clear in the size and dimension of the new linking method—so much so that, in combination with the poem's playful aspect, the whole emerges as a mock heroic.[2] There may be good thematic reasons to treat the subject matter of *The Princess* as mock heroic, but this formal character is, in retrospect, a natural development of the idyll—perhaps, given Tennyson's own playful yet epically oriented use of idyll, an inescapable one for him. Properly, *The Princess* ought to be called, not mock heroic, but idyllic-heroic, for it partakes of both genres.

The initial setting of *The Princess* is the familiar location of the English Idyls. Sir Walter Vivian's estate is the manor house already found in *Edwin Morris* and *Locksley Hall*, while the ruined abbey in which the young people take turns telling the story is reminiscent of the estate in *The Talking Oak*. The careful opposition of the sexes, apparent in the English Idyls, is used here once again, and is elevated in *The Princess* to the status of a pivotal issue. The English Idyls had presented a series of men seeking fulfillment in the world. Now Tennyson sees man as the active sex whose business is in the world, and woman as the sex above "mere social accomplishments" that, at its best, preserves, in "her imagination in its highest phases, her inborn spirituality, and her sympathy with all that is pure, noble, and beautiful," the ideal soul of humanity.[3] This division between a potentially ravenous, masculine social enterprise and the mollifying, ideal femininity that ought to guide the rapacious but sensitive male was one of the thematic links of the twelve serial idylls of 1842. When the two sexes were in perfect harmony, the result, as in *The Gardener's Daughter*, was an Eden "not wholly in the busy world, nor quite / Beyond it." The disastrous effect of sexual discord was most apparent in the narrator of *Locksley Hall* after the restraining hand of the beloved was withdrawn. *The Princess* follows the tradition of these idylls both in its locale and its perseverance in the sexual study, though it goes beyond the earlier poems in examining the possibilities inherent in the female disposition for weakness and hence for the destruction of the ideal state.

The Princess, however, not only continues the themes and forms of the earlier idylls but progresses beyond them, and it is therefore natural that one of the leading ideas of the poem should be evolution. Indeed, from *The Princess* on, evolution of one sort or another is the central preoccupation of Tennyson's poetry. It would be convenient to say that this interest grew out of Tennyson's collateral concern with the evolution of his poetic form, just as it would be to state the case in its reverse form, that his formal progress was an adjunct of his acute concern with movement in time. But in fact the situation is not reducible to either formula alone: Tennyson's formal progress and his increasing focus on the question of growth in time are inseparable issues, and to study one is to come to understand the other. *The Princess* is a poem that seeks to evolve the idyll beyond its previous Tennysonian limits of size and theme. Its complementary subject is progress in history, most especially in the relation of the sexes. The form and the theme develop together.

The almost symmetrical development of the concepts of formal poetic evolution and historical progress is apparent in the poem's leading metaphor of statuary. The first statue of many in the poem is that of Sir Ralph Vivian, "a broken statue propt against the wall" (Prologue, 99) of the ruined abbey where the storytellers spend their afternoon. The broken statue and the abbey stand in immediate contrast to the proceedings on Sir Walter's lawn, where his tenants and members of the local Scientific Institute are holding a fair. Indeed the formal, even courtly game of telling a "sevenfold story" (Prologue, 198), which the upper-class young people play, shows the same sort of contrast with the scientific games of the Institute picnickers:

> there through twenty posts of telegraph
> They flashed a suacy message to and fro
> Between the mimic stations; so that sport
> Went hand in hand with Science.   (Prologue, 77–80)

By the standards of the Scientific Institute, the storytelling in the abbey is a slow and outmoded form of communication, suited to the broken relics of the past among which it takes place. In fact, one of the formal objectives of the poem is to bring the electric mode of the picnickers and the statuelike mode of the storytellers into some sort of alignment—or if not to align these disparate modes, at least to arrange them into a medley. The Princess Ida herself states the formal goal of the poem in this regard in her lecture to her pupils about the female statuary adorning her college:

> Look, our hall!
> Our statues!—not of those that men desire,
> Sleek Odalisques, or oracles of mode,
>
> . . . . .
>
> Dwell with these, and lose
> Convention, since to look on noble forms
> Makes noble through the sensuous organism
> That which is higher.   (II, 61–63, 71–74)

Of course, Ida herself misapprehends the true import of her advice, for in the first part of the poem she is only a noble form, like the broken statue of Sir Ralph, refusing to mix her life "through the sensuous organism." Tennyson describes her at the tourney as "among the statues, statuelike" (V, 499), and her cold, alabaster performance throughout is only an extension of the metaphor. Consequently, her college ends as a noble ruin much like the abbey in which the story is told.

Not only is the Princess herself statuelike, but her manner is so stiff that life around her is also frozen by a chilly formality. Like the goddess of chastity, Artemis, with Acteaeon, the chaste Ida has the power to turn men into unnatural forms, and Tennyson uses this mythical parallel at least twice, first as a jest in Lilia's mouth in the Prologue (148–151), and again immediately after the Prince and his friends, masquerading as females, have been unmasked as men. In the ensuing confusion, the Prince is lost in the college grounds, until he

> found at length
> The garden portals. Two great statues, Art
> And Science, Caryatids, lifted up
> A weight of emblem, and betwixt were valves
> Of open-work in which the hunter rued
> His rash intrusion, manlike, but his brows
> Had sprouted, and the branches thereupon
> Spread out at top, and grimly spiked the gates.
> (IV, 182–188)

The Princess, like *The Palace of Art*, is full of statuary, though here its purpose is not purely allegorical as it was in the earlier poem. The statues are used for comic effect in the plot, as in the scene above, and stand as a metaphor for the bad metamorphosis brought about by the Princess's fixed attitudes and rigid adherence to a principle not fully in accord with the plastic impulses of nature. It is appropriate that the Prince should escape from the college grounds through the ossified horns of Acteaeon, for Acteaeon's fate awaits him if he remains. The addition of the term Caryatids, the female forms representing Art and Science, further enhances the metaphoric use of the statuary, for the Caryatids

were orginally the priestesses in the Laconian temple of Artemis. Here Tennyson links the formal and rigid program of
the college with the stony chastity of the hunting goddess,
for the paradox of Ida's curriculum is that while she has
sought to protect her female companions from any subject
that might "encarnalize their spirits" (III, 298), she has
created a lifeless discipline that turns its students into stone.
The Lady Psyche is used several times as an example of the
product of the Princess's program;[4] when she flees the college, Florian discovers her with

> brows as pale and smooth
> As those that mourn half-shrouded over death
> In deathless marble.   (V, 70–72)

Ida and her followers are more like the "bones of some
vast bulk that lived and roared / Before man was" (III,
277–278) than they themselves imagine. Far from anticipat-
ing "her that will be," the college in its isolation and rigidity
resists the natural flow of human intercourse and feeling,
and like the statue of Sir Ralph, its stony world can be
shattered. Throughout the poem Tennyson insists that re-
volt against form and convention is as rigid and fragile an
undertaking as the continuing, mindless practice of those
modes. It was a lesson he applied equally to Ida's college and
his own use of form.

In the end, however, Ida changes from a stony Artemis to
a Botticelli Venus:

> all
> Her falser self slipt from her like a robe,
> And left her woman, lovelier in her mood
> Than in her mould that other, when she came
> From barren deeps to conquer all with love;
> And down the streaming crystal dropt.   (VII, 145–150)

The cold stone turns to "streaming crystal." Like a mirror-
image Hermione, Ida is thawed from her statuelike distance
from humanity and her own lack of grace by the persistence
of the Prince's love. *The Winter's Tale*, with its statue conceit, had been on Tennyson's mind when he wrote *The*

Princess, and he mentions it in the body of the poem: "Why not a summer's as a winter's tale?" (Prologue, 204). In keeping with the reversal of the seasons, the statue conceit borrowed from Shakespeare is used in backward fashion—it is Ida who needs the grace that in *The Winter's Tale* the king requires—but Shakespeare's problem play is still an appropriate analogue for *The Princess*, not only in its statue theme, but in its mixture of genres.

Together with the Prince, the redeemed Ida now sets about to "clear away the parasitic forms" (VII, 253). Like the couple of *The Gardener's Daughter*, the combined force of Prince and Princess conspires to bring "the statelier Eden back to men" (VII, 278), not by rebellion or submission to the old, but by following the "strange diagonal" (Conclusion, 27) between these extremes: "The man be more of woman, she of man" (VII, 264).

The "strange diagonal" is the formal poetic method of *The Princess* as well, neither rebelling against the inherited forms of pastoral idyll, romance, lyric, and epic employed in its composition or wholly succumbing to their traditional structures. But this method of neither embracing nor rejecting the received poetic modes, while it preserves much of beauty in its use of tradition, also leaves the poem open to the charge of being neither fish nor fowl. Tennyson himself said of it: "though truly original, it is, after all, only a medley."[5] It was fitting that Tennyson added episodes of the Prince's seizures to the poem in its 1851 version; they maintain the close parallel between the poem's theme and its form and also highlight its odd lack of formal unity. Like the Prince, the poem is given to weird fits in which the events it describes are no longer perceived in the logic of narrative, but are shadowed forth in lyrical elements. Moreover, like the shadows of the Prince's seizures, these lyrics maintain some dim connection with the substance of the poem. The famous sequence of blank verse lyrics in Part IV, for instance, gives in miniature the whole movement of the poem from haphazard and indulgent medley toward purposeful order. The Princess and her followers are picnicking in the countryside when she calls for someone to sing. "A maid / Of those beside her" then renders the beautiful (and much anthologized) *Tears, Idle Tears*:

> Tears, idle tears, I know not what they mean,
> Tears from the depth of some divine despair
> Rise in the heart, and gather to the eyes,
> In looking on the happy Autumn-fields,
> And thinking of the days that are no more. (IV, 21–25)

F. R. Leavis condemned this lyric because "there is nothing that gives the effect of an object, or substantial independent existence" in it, and it contains "emotion for its own sake without a justifying situation."[6] The criticism is not original, for Ida makes it herself directly after the maid has finished her song:

> thine are fancies hatched
> In silken-folded idleness; nor is it
> Wiser to weep a true occasion lost,
> But trim our sails, and let old bygones be,
> While down the streams that float us each and all
> To the issue, goes, like glittering bergs of ice,
> Throne after throne, and molten on the waste
> Becomes a cloud. (IV, 48–55)

In fact, Tennyson seems to have included *Tears, Idle Tears* in *The Princess* for exactly the reasons for which Leavis condemned it—as a disembodied emotional cry for a past "without a justifying situation" in the present.

Ida, like Leavis, condemns the lyric as an unproductive exercise in sentimentalism, and Tennyson, it seems, shares her objection in that he gives little time, in *The Princess*, to pure lyric unless it is incorporated into some larger design or tradition that evolves. But because, unlike Ida, Tennyson is unwilling to scorn the lyric entirely, he strives to integrate its properties into his narrative structure. When the Prince, still in female garb, tries his hand at a lyric for Ida, the result is more appropriate to the narrative:

> O Swallow, Swallow, flying, flying South,
> Fly to her, and fall upon her gilded eaves,
> And tell her, tell her, what I tell to thee.
>
> O tell her, Swallow, thou that knowest each,
> That bright and fierce and fickle is the South,
> And dark and true and tender is the North. (IV, 75–80)

The lyric now begins to match the narrative plot, for the Prince has come from the North to woo the "fierce and fickle" Princess of the South. Ida, however, rejects his lyric as "a mere love song" (108), though she admits the possibilities of heroic and inspirational poetry:

> But great is song
> Used to great ends: ourself have often tried
> Valkyrian hymns, or into rhythm have dashed
> The passion of the prophetess; for song
> Is duer unto freedom, force and growth
> Of spirit than to junketing and love.   (IV, 119–124)

The Prince and Princess, in fact, represent the two formal strains of the poem; he inclines toward the lyric and idyllic (he fails badly in the role of heroic adventurer in the tourney —he is fashioned for wooing, not war), while she is dogmatically in favor of a loftier, wilder strain. As usual, her perspective is warped by her obsessive devotion to the principle of female advancement through disciplined isolation, but it is the Princess herself who sings the poem's most celebrated set of lyrics:

> Now sleeps the crimson petal, now the white;
> Nor waves the cypress in the palace walk;
> Nor winds the gold fin in the porphyry font:
> The fire-fly wakens: waken thou with me.
>
> Now droops the milkwhite peacock like a ghost,
> And like a ghost she glimmers on to me.
> Now lies the earth all Danaë to the stars,
> And all thy heart lies open unto me.   (VII, 161–168)

Ida's transformation from an Artemis to an Aphrodite is in part figured by her willingness, at the end, to sing the lyrics she had previously affected to despise. In her hands, at last, the lyric is not only a reflection of the narrative but an integral part of it, as in her songs to the Prince, Ida announces her change of heart. Whereas earlier in the poem her plans were all cast in Homeric orations, at the end she speaks in the Theocritean manner; her epic intentions have been mollified by a lyric tenderness:

Come down, O maid, from yonder mountain height:
What pleasure lives in height (the shepherd sang)
In height and cold, the splendor of the hills? (VII, 177–179)

Ida comes down from the college set on the mountain, and joins herself to the "true and tender" Prince of the North. At the same time the lyric, a shadow of the narrative heretofore, merges with it, just as the Prince's shadowy visions blend into the reality of the conclusion.

But while throughout the poem there is a parallelism between the shadowy lyrics and the substance of the plot, the mixed modes of the Princess remain distinct until they are conjoined at the very end. It is significant that the union of the best attributes of the sexes—which in *In Memoriam* was to be accomplished in the single figure of Hallam ("manhood fused with female grace," CIX, 17)—requires the marriage of the Prince and Ida. Throughout, *The Princess* achieves its syntheses by adding one thing to another; it never reaches the sublime and unitary vision of Tennyson's later poems. The lyrics, though in blank verse, are still lyrics, detached from the narrative. *The Princess* evolves a form in which diverse formal elements have a new and curious alliance but are not actually united. The poem certainly goes a long way beyond the idyll form Tennyson had previously used, but the form is not perfected.

The formal problem Tennyson faced was, by any standard, monumental: how to avoid the mere reproduction of the traditional genres without falling into Ida's trap of unnatural and humorless rebellion. The problem is clearly related to the idea of progress, for a poetry embodying a correct notion of growth in time must itself be part of the time scheme it describes, and its form must be evolved according to the natural and organic pattern that is the poem's theme. Ideally for Tennyson the formal progress of his poetry ought to be analogous to the evolutionary scheme that now becomes his principal theme, but judging by the form of *The Princess*, evolution is a sort of Frankenstein, patching together a "medley" of life. This solution is an advance over Tennyson's early idylls, but it is hardly an answer to either the problem of time or the problem of form. That answer was to come in *In Memoriam*.

In Memoriam

In Memoriam (1850) is in many ways a master feat of legerdemain. It purports to be—and it is—a poet's disjointed confession of faith when confronted by the death of his dearest friend; yet it is also Tennyson's most highly structured and formally innovative poem up to 1850. Since its publication, biographers and critics have rightly claimed, as Tennyson himself said, that it is his own personal statement of grief and hope following the death of Arthur Henry Hallam; yet in many aspects, *In Memoriam* is as cool and dispassionate a performance in verse as any of Tennyson's earlier dramatic monologues on classical subjects. It pretends to have—and in fact has—the spontaneity of the penitent's cry as he gropes toward faith; yet it is just as surely one of the most calculating, even heretical, poems in the English language. *In Memoriam* makes an attempt to combine the immediacy of the lyric with the playful artifice of the idyll, just as *The Princess* had done in its medley of the two forms, but in *In Memoriam* the two are wholly synthesized.

The notion that *In Memoriam* is "a diary of which we have to read every word,"[7] recording the grief and resolution of Tennyson the mourner of Hallam, is as old as the poem itself, and is of course justified by the text and the full title of the work, *In Memoriam A.H.H., Obit MDCCCXXXIII.* But it should be remembered that before publication Tennyson had considered several other titles, including *The Way of the Soul* and *Fragments of an Elegy.* In correspondence with Aubrey de Vere he referred to the poem as his "Elegies," and when Edward Fitzgerald spoke of the work in 1845 (the existence and progress of the poem was well known to Tennyson's circle), he called it "a volume of poems —elegiac—in memory of Arthur Hallam."[8] The alternative titles are revealing in their insistence on the formal aspect of the poem, for Tennyson was quite consciously producing not only a diary, which implies a free-form and rather unstructured medium, but also an experiment in elegy, or elegiac verse.

Here a distinction should be made between the two formal terms elegy and elegiac. Elegiac verse, in the ancient world, referred to a metrical formula made up of a dactylic hexameter couplet: the first line was the regular hexameter of Homer or Vergil, while the second took this base but omitted two syllables from the hexameter line, one at the caesura, the other at the end of the verse. The second half of the elegiac couplet was therefore a slightly distorted dactylic hexameter, though because it lost two syllables, the equivalent of a quantitative foot, it was and is sometimes referred to as a pentameter. The abbreviation of the second line of the elegiac couplet fitted it, in classical poetry, for both a pithier and a less formal statement than its parent form, pure dactylic hexameter. Thus elegiacs were used in a number of contexts, ranging from public address to love song, which had in common only the desire to speak more incisively and cunningly than the regular, stately grandeur of the epic hexameter permitted. Though Ovid addressed the muse Elegia as "flebilis" (weeping) and said, in the context of Tibullus' death, "a nimis ex vero nunc tibi nomen erit" ("now your name will be all too true"), later elegiac verse such as Ovid himself wrote was primarily either amatory or satiric. A further elegiac example from the *Amores* will show both tendencies:

> Arma gravi numero violentaque bella parabam
>   edere, materia conveniente modis.
>
> par erat inferior versus: risisse Cupido
>   dicitur atque unum surripuisse pedem.   (1.1.1–4)

I was preparing to provide war and armed combat in lofty numbers, the matters matched with the mode.
I had written the second line: then Cupid laughed and stole one foot away.

For the Roman poets, it was the god of love, not death, who ruled the classical elegy, and Tennyson was aware of the presiding deity in the first lines of *In Memoriam* and throughout the poem. But it is equally important to remember that "the predominant character of archaic elegy [elegy of the eighth to six centuries B.C.] is that of a public or half-public address,"[9] a consideration that will be of interest in reflecting upon Tennyson's first use of the elegiac stanza form of *In Memoriam*.

Whereas elegiac verse refers to a kind of metrical formula that was applied to a wide variety of subject matters but gradually came to be used predominately by the Romans in amatory verse, an elegy is simply a poem, usually of moderate length, in memory of the dead. The most famous classical elegies—Theocritus' first idyll, Bion's *Lament for Adonis*, Moschus' *Lament for Bion*, Vergil's fifth eclogue—are all in the stately dactylic hexameter. Elegiac verse is used in the context of what we would call elegy only in poems much shorter than these traditional elegies. As always with the use of the elegiac couplet, the poet's choice of line seems to have been dictated by a desire to make an incisive statement—virtually an epitaph. The clearest example of this is the elegiac couplet supposedly written by Plato in memory of his lover Aster (his name meant "Star"):

> Ἀστὴρ πρὶν μὲν ἔλαμπες ἐνὶ ζωοῖσιν Ἑῷος·
> νῦν δὲ θανὼν λάμπεις Ἕσπερος ἐν φθιμένοις.

Aster, you shone like the morning star among the living while you lived;
now having died, you shine like Hesperus among the dead.

Catullus used elegiac verse in his famous ten-line tribute to his dead brother, "Multas per gente et multa per aequora vectus," but when he spoke again of his brother in elegiacs in his longer "Etsi me assiduo confectum cura dolore," the poem turned, at the end of the its twenty-four lines, to love, the natural subject of Roman elegiacs.

The elegy proper is associated not with elegiac verse but with the grand style of the hexameter line, and its most celebrated classical examples are found in collections of idylls, as in Theocritus and Vergil. Milton's *Lycidas*, in tone and length, imitates the classical idyllic elegies. It remained for Gray in his *Elegy Written in a Country Churchyard* to introduce a lyric element, reminiscent of the ancient elegiac couplet, into the elegy by way of his rhyme scheme, *a b a b*, though he continued his *Elegy* in the iambic pentameter of *Lycidas*, the English meter normally used to convey the dignity of the ancient hexameter.

Throughout his life Tennyson was interested in the transformation of classical forms and meters into English equivalents. His "Attempts at Classical Metres in Quantity," a translation of parts of the *Iliad* in the quantitative meter of the original, was published in 1863, but the same interest had been apparent not only in his nearly obsessional tendency to discuss classical forms and meters over dinner but in his early work, where he experimented with elegiac verse in several forms. The most obvious examples are the *Leonine Elegiacs* of 1830 (originally entitled simply *Elegiacs*) and the early *Elegiacs* (c. 1830?), published in 1931 by Charles Tennyson. Leonine verse is a medieval addition to Latin poetics in which a syllable or syllables before the caesura rhyme with the final syllable or syllables. (St. Bernard's *De contemptu mundi* is written in this form.) At first sight, lines from Tennyson's *Leonine Elegiacs* seem very strange indeed:

> Low-throned Hesper is stayed between the two peaks; but
>   the Naiad
>   Throbbing in mild unrest holds him beneath in her breast.
> The ancient poetess singeth, that Hesperus all things
>   bringeth.
>   Smoothing the wearied mind: bring me my love, Rosalind.
> Thou comest morning or even; she cometh not morning or
>   even.
>   False-eyed Hesper, unkind, where is my sweet Rosalind?
>   (11–16)

These odd lines are in fact a very complex experiment in verse, in which rhyme is made to assume some of the functions of classical metrics, thereby making the ancient forms accessible for English poetics. The meter is that of the classical elegiac: The first line is dactylic hexameter—but what a refreshing hexameter after the textbook example, "This is the forest primeval, the murmuring pines and the hemlocks"! The second line is the hexameter repeated with two syllables removed, one at the caesura, one at the end of the line. So far, perfect classical elegiac.

The perfection of the imitation is continued even in the development of the Hesperus theme, a favorite of elegiac poets, as the pseudo-Platonic example above shows. But the rhyme also imitates the pattern of the elegiac, for it is feminine, or two-syllabled, in the regular dactylic line, but masculine, or one-syllabled (that is, shortened) in the truncated second line. The knowledge that rhyme can subsume the functions of classical meters opened many new possibilities for Tennyson, and he was fond of playing with the potential inherent in this experiment. Much could be done simply by rearranging the order of the rhymes, since each distich of the Leonine line is fairly detachable. For instance, one might take the Leonine verses of 1830,

> Barketh the shepherd-dog cheerly; the grasshopper carolleth
>   clearly;
> Deeply the wood-dove coos; shrilly the owlet halloos,

and arrange them as follows:

> Barketh the shepherd-dog cheerly;
>   Deeply the wood-dove coos;
> The grasshooper carolleth clearly;
>   Shrilly the owlet halloos.

In this version, the scheme of the verse is only transposed, but its presentation makes it feel acceptable not only as translation of classical form but as English poetry. In fact, it is part of the form Tennyson used in *Claribel* the poem that stands at the head of the juvenilia in the final recension of his collected works:

> At noon the wild bee hummeth
>   About the mossed headstone:
> At midnight the moon cometh,
>   And looketh down alone.   (11–14)

The concession to English in this transformation is that the meter has been changed from basic dactylic to basic iambic, a concession made sooner or later by all English poets.

The *In Memoriam* stanza, first used by Tennyson in three political poems of the early 1830s—*Hail Briton!*, *You*

Ask Me, Why, and *Love Thou Thy Land*—was developed about the same time as his experiments in elegiacs and seems close to them in form and spirit. In some ways, the *In Memoriam* stanza is an adaptation of the elegiac couplet to suit Tennyson's own philosophy. The internal couplet is reminiscent of the Leonine verse of 1830, and the rhymed first and last line encapsulate the whole stanza like the shell of a nut, while providing the same kind of alteration of effect that was the impetus behind the creation of the elegiac meter in the classical world. By making the stanza tetrameter instead of iambic pentameter, the traditional English meter for grand subjects, Tennyson achieved to some extent the brevity and concision that are the soul of ancient elegiacs. It is no accident that *In Memoriam* contains Tennyson's most epigrammatic and often-quoted lines; the quasi-elegiac form of the poem was intended to provide such opportunities. It is also interesting that in its earliest Tennysonian uses (*Hail Briton!*, *You Ask Me, Why*, and *Love Thou Thy Land*) the *In Memoriam* stanza was employed in the same "public or half-public address" that characterized the ancient elegiacs.

Indeed, although *In Memoriam* is the chronicle of a personal grief, it is also a very public poem, and much of its power derives from a resonance between the poem's sincere, lyric plaints and its universal, bardic utterances. Tennyson was at some pains to achieve this effect. "It must be remembered that this is a poem, *not* an actual biography," he wrote of *In Memoriam;* and in his comments on various stanzas, he refers to the first-person narrator as "the poet." Of one stanza, he said to James Knowles, "I figure myself in this, rather"—as if his presence in the poem was more the exception than the rule. The free arrangement of his personal history, in which chronological accuracy is sacrificed to poetic logic, further suggests that the poem cannot be treated simply as a diary.[10] Perhaps the poet's desire to fashion out of his personal loss a highly wrought and calculated universal statement explains the otherwise farcical proceeding of having the poem published anonymously in 1850. Since most of literary London knew the poem was Tennyson's, and his publisher, Moxon, was at pains to in-form those who did not, this particular feint has always seemed a species of false modesty. It makes more sense to treat the poem's supposed anonymity as one of its conceits: it is a poem that could be anyone's, addressed to the public at large, like classical elegiac. The uninitiate reviewer who greeted *In Memoriam* as lines "from the full heart of the widow of a military man" may have entered into the spirit of the work more than many of his wiser colleagues: "It is rather the cry of the whole human race than mine," said Tennyson.[11]

In its stanza form alone, *In Memoriam* achieves a rare fusion; it is at once elegiac in spirit and an elegy. This combination is not unprecedented—Catullus had written elegiac elegies—but nothing in the tradition of either the elegy or elegiac verse prepares the reader for the length to which Tennyson draws out his experiment in form. At first it seems a contradiction that he should have chosen a poetic form designed for concision and then extended it to almost epic proportions, but he had embarked on a journey out of the idyll, a voyage through which he hoped to shed all the restrictions of that form while maintaining what was essentially good in it. Insofar as elegy retains traditional links with idyll, *In Memoriam* is in the idyll tradition, but it is idyll stripped down for speed and rigged out to encompass a single and unified vision of life. In purely formal terms, *In Memoriam* goes a giant step beyond Shelley's *Adonais,* for Shelley's poem is in the decorous and traditional pentameter, made even more grave and ponderous by the final twelve-syllable line in each stanza, and it is only a fraction of the length of Tennyson's effort. *In Memoriam,* on the other hand, steers away from the stately aspect of elegy: its lack of pomp is an essential element in sustaining its length—if the structure were not of fairly light material, it would collapse into a morose heap. But it avoids falling into the opposite camp of rebellion against the form—Ida's weakness—because it is propped up by the elegiac stanza. *In Memoriam* finally manages what Tennyson had wanted all along: it is completely traditional and completely original at the same time.

The elegiac tradition in which Tennyson was working

was, at least in Roman usage, largely amatory, and this heritage, far from being an obstacle, seems to have suited his design for *In Memoriam* perfectly:

> Strong Son of God, immortal Love,
>   Whom we, that have not seen thy face,
>   By faith, and faith alone, embrace,
> Believing where we cannot prove;
>
> Thine are these orbs of light and shade;
>   Thou madest Life in man and brute;
>   Thou madest Death; and lo, thy foot
> Is on the skull which thou hast made.

In Memoriam is both love song and elegy, and these opening lines are nicely divided between fear and celebration.[12] In fact, these lines may be about love in a more complex way than has been thought: on the basis of Tennyson's remark that they "might be taken in a St. John sense," they are traditionally glossed as an invocation of a purely Christian love; and yet they might equally well be read as a reference to Apuleius' myth of Cupid and Psyche, in which the Soul, selected by Love as his mate, is nonetheless forbidden to look him in the face, and must accept their nuptials on faith alone. This reading of the lines is particularly appealing when extended to the whole structure of the poem, which ends with an epithalamium, as does the myth, but one only celebrated after the Soul (Tennyson had considered calling the poem *The Way of the Soul*) has been set the task of separating the "confused seeds" of faith and doubt, "which were imposed on Psyche as an incessant labor to cull out and sort asunder," as Milton has it in his *Areopagitica*. Since *In Memoriam* is a poem of syntheses, it is not surprising to find pagan and Christian myth, that of Apuleius and St. John, united in a single sense.

The use of the elegiac spirit in the elegy also allowed Tennyson, without actually breaking away from tradition, to do what would otherwise have been a complete contradiction in an elegy. *In Memoriam* is not only threnody, as in a Theocritean elegy; it is also in large measure an epithalamium, most obviously in its concluding section celebrating the marriage of Tennyson's sister Cecilia to his friend Edmund Lushington. But the final epithalamium is carefully prepared throughout the poem: marriage is a recurring theme in *In Memoriam*. At first it is a marriage dissolved by death ("Till all my widowed race be run," IX, 18, perhaps the line that befuddled the reviewer for the *Literary Gazette*), but later it is marriage as a new possibility, figured forth in the image of a young bride:

> Could we forget the widowed hour
>   And look on Spirits breathed away,
>   As on a maiden in the day
> When first she wears her orange-flower!
>
> .   .   .   .   .
>
> But thou and I have shaken hands,
>   Till growing winters lay me low;
>   My paths are in the fields I know
> And thine in undiscovered lands.   (XL, 1–4, 29–32)

The meeting of the parallel careers of living poet and dead friend is viewed, in this part of the poem, as an impossibility in earthly time. But fifty-seven stanzas later the poet sees "my spirit as of a wife" (XCVII, 8), and the epilogue completes the marriage, or rather re-marriage, on terms that the poem has established. This concluding epithalamium follows the traditional order and form of Sappho's and Catullus' epithalamia—celebration of the vows, postnuptial banquet, and finally the fertility song before the bridal chamber, in which heirs are hoped for. Tennyson, a lifelong devotee of Sappho and Catullus, paid his greatest tribute to his lyric masters in *In Memoriam* when he took their distinct traditions of elegy and epithalamium and knit them into a whole that preserved the spirit of both in a completely innovative way.

Though *In Memoriam* is not the pure lyric it has been claimed to be, it is in part lyric, for its roots lie not only in the pastoral elegy but in the lyric tradition of Sappho and Catullus. Of course, the elegiac mode and the lyric can and do intersect, both in the classical poets and in Tennyson (Catullus' "Etsi me assiduo confectum cura dolore" shows this); but in approaching *In Memoriam* it is advisable to keep the concept of lyric apart, for Tennyson at first treats it as a separate form to which he has recourse when the pastoral, idyllic elegy fails him. To Tennyson the lyric tradition was a "self-infolded" form in which the poet captured universal experience by singing about himself for an audience that, though containing many listeners, had only one critic of consequence, again himself. *In Memoriam* seems at first to be the poem par excellence that fits this highly Romantic definition of lyric. Precisely because it has been perceived as an attempt at pure lyric along these lines, it has also been condemned for not sustaining the lyric impetus.[13] *In Memoriam*, a poem driven by an almost greedy obsession to get beyond all traditional, formal models, would have failed in its purpose had it confined itself to any one form. Rather, out of the variety of forms with which it experiments—pastoral, elegy, idyll, elegiac verse, lyric, epithalamium, psalm, and even at one point epic—it seeks to evolve a new form that sacrifices nothing of the past (just as none of Hallam's earthly stay is sacrificed to the destroyer, time) while at the same time representing a distinct advance upon the whole tradition.

The evolutionary question, rightly perceived to be at the heart of *In Memoriam*, is not present in the poem simply as a by-product of the scientific speculation of the nineteenth century as applied to the particular case of Arthur Hallam's death. This contention, which is indisputably borne out by the substance of the poem, has habitually afforded critics a textual crux, for *In Memoriam* was published nine years before Darwin's *Origin of Species*, and its major sections on evolution predated Robert Chambers's *Vestiges of Creation*.[14] In the absence of evidence to link Tennyson with these seminal works, it has been supposed either that he drew his startlingly rounded conception of the evolutionary debate from Charles Lyell's *Principles of Geology* (1830), which he read in 1837, or that he was intuitively conscious of the central idea permeating the Victorian *Zeitgeist*. Both these assertions may be true, as well as Charles Tennyson's that the poet "closely and anxiously followed" the parallel evolutionary developments of the higher criticism in Germany and of liberalism in England.[15] But it is not necessary to go so far afield to find Tennyson's paramount evolutionary interest: at least from his college days and perhaps before them, he had been preoccupied with the question of the movement and progress of literary form, and his whole career may be said to have been a struggle with this issue. Tennyson's evolutionary interest was the self-centered interest of the craftsman, though certainly this fundamental concern embraced the whole range of evolutionary questions posed by the various disciplines in the nineteenth century.

Tennyson's interest in the evolution of form was at least as old as Hallam's review of his 1830 volume, "On Some of the Characteristics of Modern Poetry, and on the Lyrical Poems of Alfred Tennyson," in which he asserts that Tennyson has created "a new species [later the central Darwinian term] of poetry, a graft of the lyric on the dramatic, and Mr. Tennyson deserves the laurel of an inventor, an enlarger of our modes of knowledge and power."[16] Although Hallam's praise was premature in this instance (Tennyson was not yet inventing a form, but rather rediscovering the idyll), the underlying concept was a very exact appraisal of the Tennysonian program: his interest in the "species" of poetry, his impulse to "graft" one species upon another, and his desire to innovate within the tradition. It is fitting that these attributes, which Hallam so admired, later found their most intricate expression in the poem dedicated to his memory. And it is not surprising that for Tennyson, whose life was centered on his poetic craft, the genesis of evolutionary interest should have been a craftsman's dilemma.

Hallam's observations on the evolutionary and innovative nature of Tennyson's poetry were not made in a critical void, nor were Tennyson's formal experiments of 1830 or 1850. August Schlegel had stated the Romantic position on the development of genre in 1808: "poetry, as the fervid expression of our whole being, must assume new and peculiar forms in different ages." Chateaubriand in *Le Génie du christianisme* (1802) and Hugo in his preface to *Cromwell* (1827) had infused this dictum with a plangent note asserting that the emotion dominating Schlegel's "expression of our whole being" in the new age was "plus que la gravité et moins que la tristesse, la mélancolie," and that to express this new emotion poetry would assume new types and forms: "Ce type c'est le grotesque. Cette forme, c'est la comédie."[17] The veneration of this European spirit of *innovation mélancolique*, which, unlike its English cognate, denotes a kind of peaceful, rapturous contemplation upon the vagaries of human life, is apparent in Arthur Hallam's criticism, and it also found its way into *In Memoriam*. Hallam had written of Dante,

> An English mind that has drunk deep at the sources of Southern inspiration, and especially that is imbued with the spirit of the mighty Florentine, will be conscious of a perpetual freshness and quiet beauty resting on his imagination and spreading gently over his affections, until, by the blessing of heaven, it may be absorbed without loss, in the pure inner light, of which that voice has spoken as no other can.[18]

Hallam's description of the spirit of Dante is an English equivalent of Hugo's and Chateaubriand's *mélancolie*, which probably could not have been written without the French influence. It is also an excellent description of the spirit that later imbued *In Memoriam*, a poem evolved along the lines Hugo imagined the new literature would take: *la comédie mélancolique*.[19]

But Hallam's remarks on the "quiet beauty" that he hoped would infuse English poetry were made not about Romanticism but about the Italian Renaissance. This distinction was not only crucial for Hallam, but it is crucial for an appreciation of Tennyson's approach to tradition. The literature of the Italian Renaissance might have, for Hallam, the revolutionary qualities that Schlegel and Hugo discerned as the marks of formal evolution, but it possessed these in conjunction with its "capacity of taking into itself, into its own young and creative vigor, the whole height, breadth, and depth of human knowledge, as it then stood."[20] True literary innovation did not therefore reject what had gone before but incorporated it, and the model for this innovation was the literature of the Trecento. Hallam's indebtedness to the Italian Renaissance is well known. It is sometimes cited as an influence upon Tennyson's thinking, which it undoubtedly was, but Tennyson's independent knowledge and use of the Italian tradition should not be overlooked.

Tennyson knew Italian long before he met Hallam—at twelve he quoted Dante to his aunt in a letter—and his well-known remark that *In Memoriam* was "a sort of Divine Comedy" came from a long acquaintance with the literature of the Italian Renaissance.[21]

This knowledge is helpful in understanding *In Memoriam* not only because Tennyson compared the movement of the poem to that of the *Divina Commedia* (many other works share a progress out of the depths toward a happy close), but because the poem's formal organization seems rooted partially in the critical theory of the Romantic movement and particularly of the Trecento. Though *In Memoriam* is a *comédie mélancolique* in the sense of French, and in part of German, Romanticism, it is not a revolutionary poem in the spirit of the Romantic movement. Romanticism was a movement of credos announcing their breaks with the past; whether these breaks were in fact capable of being effected, or even seriously intended, was not essential. Tennyson's whole philosophy of poetry ran directly counter to such credos, for he sought a formal accommodation by which poetry might move forward without sacrificing anything in the tradition, as Hallam imagined the Trecento had done. This is the formal objective of *In Memoriam*, and it coincides to perfection with the poem's theme, which is the preservation of the dead beloved, entire and intact, in the flux of time.

While the theme of *In Memoriam* may be like that of Dante's *Commedia*, its formal structure more closely resembles *La Vita nuova*; and its place in the Tennysonian canon is analogous to that of Dante's multiform experiment in relation to his epic of hell, purgatory, and heaven.[22] The similarity resides in a wide variety of elements: both *In Memoriam* and *La Vita nuova* concern the loss of a beloved who becomes the focus of a larger discussion of universal harmony; both works insist that the struggle toward this harmony is at least mirrored by, and perhaps equivalent to, the poetic endeavor of bringing formal organization to the work at hand; and both works must organize many disparate forms in order to reach the poetic and spiritual harmony toward which they move. (It is interesting that one of Tennyson's copies of Dante's canzone and sonnets

is also one of the very few books from his library that bears
an inscription in Hallam's hand.)[23] Just as *La Vita nuova* is
a curious mixture of love song and elegy delivered with un-
deniable personal involvement and including a detached, almost academic self-reflective excursus on the literary properties of the work in prograss, so *In Memoriam* reaches its
conclusion only after a series of confrontations with both
grief and form.

A. C. Bradley's celebrated division of Tennyson's poem
into four parts, punctuated by the Christmas sections expanding upon the loss of Hallam and the mourner's continuing efforts to come to terms with his bereavement, is
shadowed by another parallel division. Before each of Bradley's breaks, the poet invariably introduces sections that discuss form. In the first part of the poem, the speaker confronts
a paradoxical dilemma concerning death and change, in
which these states either produce anarchic fluctuations that
might have

> made me that delirious man
> Whose fancy fuses old and new,
> And flashes into false and true
> And mingles all without a plan   (XVI, 17–20)

or alternatively only seem to produce these effects because
sorrow masks an unchanging state that

> knows no more of transient form
> In her deep self, than some dead lake
>
> That holds the shadow of a lark
> Hung in the shadow of a heaven.[24]   (XVI, 7–10)

The world either is in unending Heraclitean flux or is frozen
in Parmenidean unity, leading in the first instance to lunatic
and senseless alterations or in the second to a dead and stag-
nant universe. In this section of the poem, the Parmenidean
alternative is rejected through the use, and eventual tran-
scendence, of the pastoral mode, which, as the oldest form
of the elegy proper, represents a tradition that "knows no
more of transient form" and continues its practices without
change down through the centuries.

For several stanzas Tennyson assumes the garb of the pastoral idyllist and, in confronting the question central to his early career—whether it is possible to move beyond the idyll form—comes to the larger question of whether change is illusory:

> I sing to him that rests below,
>> And, since the grasses round me wave,
>> I take the grasses of the grave,
> And make them pipes whereon to blow.   (XXI, 1–4)

This pastoral mood is continued in the "happy Pan" and "flute of Arcady" references of stanza XXIII,[25] and Tennyson proclaims that he sings the traditional pastoral elegy, which at this point *In Memoriam* seems to be the dominant mode of the poem, out of a natural compulsion or necessity: "I do but sing because I must, / And pipe but as the linnets sing" (XXI, 23–24). This pastoral metaphor asserts that the pastoral is the inescapable form for lamentation, just as time, death, and grief are the inescapable eventualities of life. Here the poem seems to have embraced a gloomy Parmenideanism asserting that what is, has already been and must forever be.

If *In Memoriam* rested on this outlook the poem would not need to continue beyond its earliest sections. But the fatalistic traditionalism of the first part is rejected at precisely the point identified by Bradley as the end of the poem's first division:

> I envy not in any moods
>> The captive void of noble rage,
>> The linnet born within the cage,
> That never knew the summer woods:
>
> I envy not the beast that takes
>> His license in the field of time,
>> Unfettered by the sense of crime,
> To whom a conscience never wakes;
>
> Nor, what may count itself as blest,
>> The heart that never plighted troth
>> But stagnates in the weeds of sloth;
> Nor any want-begotten rest.

> I hold it true, whate'er befall;
> I feel it, when I sorrow most;
> 'Tis better to have loved and lost
> Than never to have loved at all. (XXVII, 1–16)

Tennyson returns to the pastoral linnet, but now imagines it not as a natural, if deterministic, creature, but as a prisoner, unnaturally confined. The pastoral is seen as a restricting form that, even at the price of suffering, must be overcome, and the stagnating "dead lake" of Section XVI is rejected as a false view of life, along with "the weeds of sloth" it engenders. Yet this rejection is not triumphant:

> Make one wreath more for Use and Wont,
> That guard the portals of the house;
>
> Old sisters of a day gone by,
> Gray nurses, loving nothing new;
> Why should they miss their yearly due
> Before their time? They too will die. (XXIX, 11–16)

The universe then is Heraclitean: "all things will die." Tennyson's verses themselves are poetic wreaths in which the ancient forms are commemorated even as they wind down to their inevitable dissolution, with the extrinsically loose structure of *In Memoriam* heightening this sense of disintegration.

The poet, now aware that, like Hallam, the traditional forms must perish, struggles in the second division of the poem (up to Section LXXIII) to find some new means of expression beyond the traditional elegy, just as he is searching to know what form Hallam himself has attained in the life beyond the veil. At first, the quest for new form seems hopeless and anarchic: in a world of pure flux such as he imagines, there is no absolute upon which to rest either one's faith or one's creativity:

> This round of green, this orb of flame,
> Fantastic beauty; such as lurks
> In some wild Poet, when he works
> Without a conscience or an aim. (XXXIV, 5–8)

Here, as throughout, the structure of the universe and the organization of the poem are treated as one. The poet feels himself unable to sing either a coherent or an intelligible song in the universe he has so far envisioned—his Melpomene is "but an earthly Muse" who "darkened sanctities with song" (XXXVII, 13, 24)—and in all the poetic stock of his trade, there lives only "a doubtful gleam of solace" (XXXVIII, 8). Such misgivings continue throughout this division of the poem, but here, in Section XL, Tennyson introduces as a leitmotif the wedding theme of the "maiden in the day / When first she wears her orange-flower." The theme comes to dominate the poem as the early elegy sections turn into the concluding epithalamium, by much the same process as Hallam is converted into an enduring creature of eternal beauty. This formal process of change imitates the conversion of the caterpillar into the butterfly. The poet pretends to be unconscious of the potential in the theme he has introduced, but the reader should not be. "Thou art turned to something strange" (XLI, 5), the poet says of his dead beloved, and consciously or not, his poem is undergoing a like metamorphosis.

This metamorphosis is not easy, for at first the poet's sorrow dares not "trust a larger lay" (XLVIII, 13), an expression perhaps taken from Vergil's announcement in his fourth eclogue of his intention to sing "paulo maiore," "somewhat larger." The context of the borrowing is entirely appropriate to Tennyson's purpose, for it is his aim to break out of the idyll into the larger vision of some new form, as Vergil had done, and phrases reminiscent of Vergil's proclamation dot his text from this point on: his Muse promises him "a nobler leave" of his dead friend (LVIII, 12); he will sing with "fresher throat" (LXXXIII, 16); in time he becomes "the fuller minstrel" (CVI, 20); and eventually the poem is carried away on "a fuller wave" (CXXII, 12). But in Bradley's second division of the poem the larger song is an unfulfilled desire, and the poet is full of dubiety. His song is "but a cry" (LIV, 20), and the strictures applied to nature pertain equally to the literary tradition. When he says of nature, "So careful of the type she seems, / So careless of the single life" (LV, 7–8), he is also stating that while the forms of literature expressing the inmost feeling of humanity seem to abide, the feeling itself and the living personality behind it are lost: "But I shall pass, my work will fail" (LVII, 8). The Muse at this point encourages the poet to persevere—"Abide a little longer here, / And thou shalt take a nobler leave" (LVIII, 11–12)—and the poet dutifully returns to his efforts to construct an elegy, this time producing a very credible imitation of Gray's *Churchyard* elegy, in which even the diction is reminiscent of his eighteenth-century model:

> Dost thou look back on what hath been,
>   As some divinely gifted man,
>   Whose life in low estate began
> And on a simple village green;
>
>   . . . . .
>
> Who ploughs with pain his native lea
>   And reaps the labour of his hands,
>   Or in the furrow musing stands;
> "Does my old friend remember me?"
>   (LXIV, 1–4, 25–28)

Tennyson's borrowings are rarely accidental. Here he evokes Gray only to reject his advances in elegy as incommensurate with the difficulties he himself faces in his threnody. In the dreams that now besiege the poet through several sections he faces complexities that Gray's plaintive tones cannot answer; the voice of the dead man he hears in his visions "was not the voice of grief, / The words were hard to understand" (LXIX, 19–20). Gray's form of elegy will not suffice any more than the pastoral mode did earlier, for the poet confronts a situation in which he can barely discern the sense of what he must sing.

To bring order to his dreams and visions, Tennyson discards the conventions of pastoral and elegy and turns to the lyric mode. The traditional poetic quest is abjured; instead of either singing the praise of the dead man or enshrining his memory in literary forms of dubious longevity and effect, the poet turns inward, using for his own purposes all the glory that would have been Hallam's had he lived.

The Fuller Minstrel

> O hollow wraith of dying fame,
>   Fade wholly, while the soul exalts,
>   And self-infolds the large results
> Of force that would have forged a name.
>
> (LXXIII, 13–16)

If time brings an end to all men and to all the conventions, literary or otherwise, by which they seek to perpetuate themselves, then the traditional forms of poetry, at least at this point in the poem, are vanity. Only the true lyric, singing of itself to itself, makes any sense, for it has no claim or ambition beyond its power of assuaging present grief—and in this philosophical scheme only the present is important. The poet has struggled through the received poetic tradition only to reject it in favor of a completely self-centered form, and he concludes his second division of the poem with this Romantic revelation:

> What hope is here for modern rhyme
>   To him, who turns a musing eye
>   On songs, and deeds, and lives, that lie
> Foreshortened in the tract of time?
>
> These mortal lullabies of pain
>   May bind a book, may line a box,
>   May serve to curl a maiden's locks;
> Or when a thousand moons shall wane
>
> A man upon a stall may find,
>   And passing, turn the page that tells
>   A grief, then changed to something else
> Sung by a long-forgotten mind.
>
> But what of that? My darkened ways
>   Shall ring with music all the same;
>   To breathe my loss is more than fame,
> To utter love more sweet than praise. (LXXVII, 1–16)

The acceptance of this Romantic credo is no easier than the rejection of the pastoral was at the end of the poem's first division, and it is followed by the poet's own rebuke of the implied selfishness of the Romantic position: "O last regret, regret can die!" But the rebuke is immediately answered with the assurance that this is not so:

No—mixt with all this mystic frame
   Her deep relations are the same,
   But with long use her tears are dry.
                    (LXXVIII, 16–20)

The old forms live on side by side with the new, "self-infolded" spirit at work in the poet. Thus in the third division of *In Memoriam* the Romantic lyricism is grafted onto the old forms to produce a union that preserves the old while moving forward, as is necessary in the universe of flux so far envisioned:

I wage not any feud with Death
   For changes wrought on form and face;
   No lower life that earth's embrace
May breed with him, can fright my faith.

Eternal process moving on,
   From state to state the spirit walks;
   And these are but the shattered stalks,
Or ruined chrysalis of one.   (LXXXII, 1–8)

The rest of the poem is not a battle but an accommodation between the poet and "eternal process," a phrase that nicely captures the synthesis for which Tennyson is striving. In his view the formal order of the universe must account for the Heraclitean "process," while at the same time having about it an "eternal," Parmenidean dimension; the first part of this equation is reality; the second is necessary in order to make any sense of life.[26]

The business of this synthesis occupies the poet throughout Bradley's third division. Having stated his program, he immediately reintroduces the pastoral elements earlier discarded, for now the pastoral tradition and the Romantic lyric can be made to coexist:

Wild bird, whose warble, liquid sweet
   Rings Eden through the budded quicks,
   O tell me where the senses mix,
   O tell me where the passions meet,

Whence radiate: fierce extremes employ
   Thy spirits in the darkening leaf,
   And in the inmost heart of grief
   Thy passion clasps a secret joy:

And I—my harp would prelude woe—
I cannot all command the strings;
The glory of the sum of things
Will flash along the chords and go.
(LXXXVIII, 1–12)

Because Tennyson is never comfortable with a purely lyric mode, it is not surprising to find him, after the outburst of Section LXXVII, returning speedily to the tradition that had been his solace. But now the pastoral tradition, which had failed him in the poem's first division, is reconstituted in a loftier vein, promising to sing "the glory of the sum of things" as idyll never could; and the poet, while still not in full control of his new form, has nevertheless advanced well beyond the despondent sense of the earlier sections, of having lost control over his medium. This new pastoral form, modified by the poet's lyrical retreat upon himself, has in fact undergone a sea change. Whereas traditional pastoral idyll from Theocritus to Gray looked to the past and reverenced the dead, ending in epitaph (Tennyson alludes to his own use of this form as "My old affection of the tomb," LXXXV, 75), the poet's new form looks to the future and to the blending of things ("the senses mix," "the passions meet"). It is not the dead Hallam he now addresses, but the Hallam who is and is to be:

Come, beauteous in thine after form,
And like a finer light in light.   (XCI, 15–16)

As he writes, *In Memoriam* itself is assuming the aspect of an "after form." The fusion of lyric and idyll is completed in the mystical Section XCV when Hallam, the objective subject of traditional elegy, and the poet, the lyrical narrator singing of himself and for himself, are merged:

The dead man touched me from the past,
And all at once it seemed at last
The living soul was flashed on mine,

And mine in this was wound, and whirled
About empyreal heights of thought
And came on that which is, and caught
The deep pulsations of the world.   (XCV, 33–40)

This is now a poetry of universal vision. The old forms have not been rejected, but used as a medium toward a higher mode of expression, and the poet, in the sections in which he bids farewell to his Somersby home, also takes leave of the tradition he has incorporated and surpassed:

> I turn to go: my feet are set
> To leave the pleasant field and farms;
> They mix in one another's arms
> To one pure image of regret.   (CII, 21–24)

Regret is no longer the subject of anxiety it had been in earlier sections, but a pure image, fully assimilated, to be left behind while the poet and his poem move on.

Whereas Milton's *Lycidas* ended with the promise of "pastures new," *In Memoriam* leaves the pastoral idyll behind and continues past its moment of synthesis to demonstrate the scope and power of the new revelation about form. In the last section of this third division, Tennyson embarks on an epic vision; he sees Hallam in a dream, but "a summons from the sea" (CIII, 16) calls him away from the dead man. This whole section calls to mind three epic scenes, Odysseus' and Aeneas' descents into hell and the end of Tennyson's own *Morte d' Arthur,* from which Tennyson borrowed the boat carrying the dead Arthur and the accompanying maidens. Tennyson now feels that he has "waxed in every limb" (30), and indeed, it is here that he becomes "the fuller minstrel" who will formally be rung in at Section CVI. The maidens, clearly representing the poet's own creative powers, are almost left behind as Tennyson embraces his friend in his "after form," but Hallam says to them, "Enter likewise ye / And go with us" (51–52). The powers that served Tennyson in the past and the forms in which they worked are not to be lost; the future upon which he is embarking in his dream is not a repudiation of the past but a continuation of it. Appropriately, he uses references to the epic to make his point. The epic has traditionally been the form toward which idyll grows, and by invoking it now, Tennyson brings full circle what had begun as an elegy couched in the form of pastoral idyll. As the epic is naturally evolved from idyll, the Hallam who is revealed in the poet's vision is naturally evolved from the earthly man.

The forms employed in *In Memoriam*, then, are analogous in their deployment to the evolution of the human species, which "may rise on stepping-stones / Of their dead selves to higher things" (I, 3–4).[27] Hallam does not escape time, but ascends through it to his "after form," which includes all he had been in time and more. Tennyson's description of the movement of Hallam, and all things in time, might be summarized in Alfred North Whitehead's definition of change in his philosophy of organism: "Change is the description of the adventures of eternal objects in the evolving universe of actual things."[28] Likewise, Tennyson does not escape tradition, but rises slowly through it till his poetry gradually assumes the shape of an "after form," partaking of the pastoral idyll, the classicl elegy, the elegiac mode, the lyric, and then the highest traditional form, the epic. In the last of Bradley's divisions of the poem, this painful ascent to higher form is celebrated at length. Gone are the pastoral "mask and mime": "For change of place, like growth of time, / Has broke the bond of dying use" (CV, 10–12). The festivity that follows, and that ends in epithalamium, is not for those who "keep an ancient form / Through which the spirit breathes no more" (CV, 19–20), but for those who have moved through the lower forms to the new institutions that both incorporate and replace the old. This last division of the poem institutes new, evolved forms in all the areas with which the poet has been concerned. Traditional genre is replaced, and with it go the "ancient forms of party strife" (CVI, 14).

But most important, of course, is the new spiritual order that is introduced, for the poem now sets about to "ring in the Christ that is to be" (CVI, 32). *In Memoriam* is often hailed—or denounced—as an epitome of Christian faith, which is to ignore the obvious conclusion of Tennyson's general statements about forms. If formal developments relentlessly subsume and supersede earlier forms, and if nothing is immune from this process, neither genres nor humanity, then Christianity itself is but a stepping-stone; something higher awaits beyond it, and Tennyson is bold enough to be the prophet of that something in *In Memoriam*. Immediately after he has celebrated the last Christmas of the poem, and sung of "the Christ who is to be," he turns to the birth of Hallam:

It is the day when he was born.

. . . . .

> We keep the day, with festal cheer,
>   With books and music; surely we
>   Will drink to him, whate'er he be,
> And sing the songs he loved to hear. (CVII, 1, 21–24)

Hallam, or rather what Hallam has come to represent—a humanity evolved to perfection through an organic though painful process—is the new Christ. This Tennysonian assertion is a startling piece of heresy, but nothing in Tennyson's poetry or life contradicts it. Tennyson not only rejected the idea of Christ's Incarnation as a central, one-time event to which all human history would be bound, but he instituted a belief, fully expressed in the themes and forms of *In Memoriam*, that the Incarnation was in fact an "eternal process," continuing forever in every birth. Tennyson is careful in his handling of this heresy, and he seems to have been sufficiently cautious to elude censure in his own day; but the heresy is there nonetheless.[29]

Having evolved new poetic and spiritual forms out of the old, with the figure of Hallam at their head, Tennyson now begins to exercise the power of his new poetic. The parts of *In Memoriam* with the strongest Biblical influences are the last sections that sing the new religion: in Section CVIII Tennyson imitates Psalm 139 ("If I ascend up into heaven, thou are there: if I make my bed in hell, behold, thou art there"):

> What profit lies in barren faith,
>   And vacant yearning, though with might
>   To scale the heaven's highest height,
> Or dive below the wells of Death?
>
> What find I in the highest place,
>   But mine own phantom changing hymns?
>   And on the depths of death, there swims
> The reflex of a human face.   (CVIII, 5–12)

It is no longer the Christian God who is found in the psalmist's flight, but the reflex of self and humanity, the image of the new religion. Under the influence of Hallam,

who is now the god of process, the new faith will flourish
and the struggle for order, a central conceit of the poem,
will be achieved. The poet says of Hallam,

> For what wert thou? some novel power
>> Sprang up for ever at a touch,
>> And hope could never hope too much
> In watching thee from hour to hour,
>
> Large elements in order brought,
>> And tracts of calm from tempest made,
>> And world-wide fluctuation swayed
> In vassel tides that followed thought.   (CXII, 9–16)

Under the discipline of this new dispensation, the poet has
at last found a principle by which the "large elements" of
his poem are "in order brought." The forms comprising
the poem, though "seeming-random" (CXVIII, 10), are
in fact caught up in universal system:

> I see in part
> That all, as in some piece of art,
> Is toil cooperant to an end.   (CXXVIII, 22–24)

In the concluding epithalamium, the poem both cele-
brates this universal cooperation in the form most fitting
for the union of disparate members, and demonstrates the
new formal scheme that is the poem's revelation. For just
as *In Memoriam* daringly asserts a new spirituality with a
representative Hallam at its head, it also dissolves the rigid
theory of poetic genres in which Tennyson initially felt himself trapped. An elegy that ends in an epithalamium is certainly of a new order, though like the universal order Tennyson envisions, it is built of the detritus of the ancient forms.

SIX

The Various World: Tennyson's Epic Vision

THOUGH *In Memoriam* was in many respects a public artifact, it was also autobiographical: in structure it was a replica of the experiments and conclusions with regard to form that made up Tennyson's career. He was loathe to leave his building block, the idyll, behind, even when he realized that his vision of "Universal Nature moved by Universal Mind" required a larger medium of expression. Typically, he found a way of preserving what was basic in his concept of idyll as he pushed beyond the genre. In *In Memoriam* by engrafting upon the idyll form elements of various lyric forms and extending the whole to epic length until he stretched the fabric of the idyll to the breaking point, he had achieved a poetic mode of expression capable of extended flight. The rest of his career consisted in large measure of testing the reborn idyll form against the materials of the Arthurian legend in *The Idylls of the King*. But before he began this culminating endeavor, he made one last effort to consolidate and refine the conclusions of *In Memoriam* in his poem *Maud* (1854).

Maud

Maud is that "new species of poetry, a graft of the lyric on the dramatic," that Arthur Hallam had discerned in the volume of 1830. It could only appear as a new species, however, after the experiment with lyric and idyll in *In Me-*

moriam. While *Maud* firmly builds on the convention of the dramatic monologue (Tennyson liked the epithet "mono-drama," in which the dramatic and idyllic strains of the poem are reckoned, and adopted it as the poem's subtitle),[1] it moves well beyond that convention in anticipation of the form that would be needed for the Arthurian epic.

The distinction of *Maud* as a dramatic monologue is not merely its length or its incorporation of lyric but the variety of mental states it portrays. Before *Maud*, the idyll as mono-logue had always been the depiction of some one psychic or emotional state, objectively described by the poet through the mouth of someone speaking in the first person. In this respect the monologue had borne a close resemblance to a Theophrastian character sketch. In his early idyll sequences, Tennyson had imitated Vergil, and perhaps Theocritus, in setting a number of these sketches side by side in a significant order to achieve a broader range of human types; but he had not then solved the problem of how to achieve this kind of breadth in a single work. He found the solution partially in *In Memoriam*, where a lyric element was intro-duced to display the speaker's changing emotional states, and this lyric element was finally wedded to the idyll form in a unified poetry capable of tackling a variety of human moods and attitudes—from elation to despair, from faith to skepticism—within a single medium. In *Maud*, this mar-riage of lyric and idyll is applied in yet a more concrete way than in *In Memoriam*, where the poet had confronted a situation—the loss of his beloved—left purposely nebulous in order that it might be more general. In other words, *In Memoriam* sacrificed the traditional plot, or setting, or whatever concrete trappings go into the making of idyll—in *Ulysses*, for example, these trappings are our knowledge of the legend and the very real presence of the hero in Ithaca—for a lyric universality in order to encompass the poem's wider vision. In *Maud*, Tennyson tries to incorporate the same range of vision within a traditionally concrete idyll framework. The speaker cannot now be mistaken for "the widow of a military man"; he is a character modeled, with some modifications, on the speakers of the idylls *Edwin Morris* and *Locksley Hall*. His problem is not the generalized anguish triggered by the death of the beloved as in *In Me-*

moriam, but a specific neurosis with concrete causes that admits of a practical cure. Unlike the situation in *In Memoriam*, where the cure is spiritual, the speaker in *Maud*, who would presumably have been healed of his misery by the love of Maud, had she lived, is actually healed by his embrace of "the blood-red blossom of war" (III, 53).

In *Maud*, Tennyson chose to reinvest his poetry with plot—a medium using identifiable characters involved in a coherent sequence of actions amid concrete landscapes. This, perhaps more than any other choice he made during his poetic career, has tarnished his reputation in our century, and has led to the false conclusion that he was primarily a moral poet, morality being considered the ineluctable result of a poetry of plot.[2] But his choosing to use the formal innovations of *In Memoriam* in connection with concrete subject matter was at the least an instinctive action on Tennyson's part, and at best an inspired strategy. He had already pushed the lyrical idyll to its limits in *In Memoriam*. Anything longer would require more of the concrete; anything more subjective developed at such length would alienate or befuddle even a small, sympathetic audience. (Hart Crane's brilliant, boring *The Bridge* is a later example of what Tennyson wished to avoid in this regard.)

Tennyson's use of the lyric and idyllic forms of *In Memoriam* to tell the plot of *Maud* was no accident, for at that point in his career he was planning his modern epic, *The Idylls of the King*, in which the shorter forms of emotional intensity would be combined with the longer forms of narrative development. *Maud* was a trial run in this process, and Tennyson's attraction to a poetry with plot was motivated by the same reasoning that had led Vergil and Milton to it earlier: the shorter forms are capable of describing the various mental or emotional states that constitute life, but the longer narrative forms traditionally show how these states are linked, not only in one mind, but in the relations of men with men and men with nature. The depiction of these relations working themselves out in time gives narrative poetry both its universality and its plot.

Maud was the artist's preliminary sketch for the union of idyllic sensibility with narrative structure. Its hero moves through a series of mental attitudes and concrete actions, which are closely connected. He begins his prolonged monologue in isolation and in a state of dithyrambic involution: "What! Am I raging alone as my father raged in his Mood?" (I, 53). From this morbid state he moves to a pastoral rapport with himself and the world, achieved through the love of Maud:

> There is none like her, none.
> Nor will be when our summers have deceased.
> O, art thou sighing for Lebanon
> In the long breeze that streams to the delicious East,
> Sighing for Lebanon,
> Dark cedar, though thy limbs have here increased,
> Upon a pastoral slope as fair,
> And looking to the South, and fed
> With honeyed rain and delicate air,
> And haunted by the starry head
> Of her whose gentle will has changed my fate,
> And made my life a perfumed altar-flame.   (I, 611–622)

After Maud's death he moves again through madness; but he finally finds solace, not in the pastoral, but in the heroic: "myself have awakened, as it seems, to the better mind; / It is better to fight for the good than to rail at the ill" (III, 56–57). Each of these mental states has its concrete counterpart in the actions of the hero in the poem's unfolding plot. Tennyson sought to bring unity to the hero's diverse actions and attitudes by two formal devices: first, the whole poem is couched in the dramatic-monologue form (the poet's favorite form of idyll); and second, the hero's various mental states—and they range from seething madness through lyrical adoration of Maud to martial declamation—are presented in a consistent metrical blend of anapests and iambs. Later, in *The Idylls of the King*, Tennyson the craftsmen would try to create a single meter capable of expressing the whole range of human emotion. He had already tried a similar experiment in *Maud*, by fashioning around one monologue in the idyll tradition a coherent narrative both of mental states and of actions resulting from them, unified by formal devices.

In *Maud*, then, Tennyson began to apply the fusion of forms used in *In Memoriam* to concrete subject matter, an application that would culminate in *The Idylls of the King*. No longer was the idyll a one-dimensional representation of single human states; it had become multifaceted as the result of the lyric infusion. As Tennyson himself said of *Maud*, "The peculiarity of this poem is that different phases of passion in one person take the place of different characters." These different phases are admissible not by virtue of the poem's alternations of meter and tone, though these are the means to the end and have their own consistency, but by virtue of its willingness to look behind the statement of its speaker to the lyrical sources of his speech and action.[3] Tennyson's Ulysses could hardly have paused in mid-sentence while a lyrical bubble in praise of home and family rose to the surface of his text. Such an action would have made him seem irresolute, even weak, though it might have given the reader a more accurate picture of his state of mind. But this was exactly the plan of *Maud:* to allow all the working of the mind—not simply its public, or concluded reasoning (though this too is part of the poem)—to come forth, usually in the poem's lyrics, used here to describe the most private, most basic working of the human psyche. To juxtapose the formal statement of the traditional idyll with the lyrical subtext that occasions it is the only way to make sense of *Maud*, for the lyric provides the clue for understanding the narrator. Taken alone, for instance, the speech in the first thirty-five lines of Part II, beginning, "The fault was mine, the fault was mine," is the fevered involution of a mind demonstrably unbalanced, yet trying to make a rational, public statement. But taken with the famous lyric that precedes it, "Come into the garden, Maud," the actions described in the speech and its rhetoric are both understandable: the lover's private yearning for serenity and harmony has been thwarted by the brothers' intrusion into the garden, and the objectively melodramatic scene that follows must be weighed in the light of the pain the speaker feels at the interruption of his lyrical vision.

Given such a vehicle for rounding out its hitherto unitary perspective, the idyll form would never again need to be a static presentation. It could be a fluid, mental drama with a plot of sorts, and the characters through which it speaks could forever be retrieved from any moral judgment (such as had fallen on Tennyson's Ulysses), because their actions and statements would be seen not as reasoned choices but as the outcome of certain preexisting states of mind. Modern poetry owes a great deal to this formal development. T. S. Eliot borrowed the form of *Maud* for his *Wasteland*, as well as one of its lines for the keynote of his poem.[4] The rounded vision, in which moral judgment is suspended in favor of psychological description, had been pioneered in Tennyson's poem; indeed, even the Bradleian conclusion reached by Eliot, that humans live in unreasoning and unreasonable capsules of isolation, is present in *Maud*, though Tennyson and Eliot go their separate ways from this premise. In *In Memoriam*, Tennyson knew his God of love "by faith alone" and created a new form to express Him. The mood in *Maud*, which is akin to this, is perhaps best expressed in the lines from its pendant piece, *The Charge of the Light Brigade*, written at the same time. Tennyson has frequently been ridiculed for writing this poem, but its sentiment is a logical outgrowth of *In Memoriam* and *Maud*. The soldiers are noble because

> Their's not to make reply,
> Their's not to reason why,
> Their's but to do and die.   (13–15)

In a universe not amenable to the connective powers of reason, they have yet found a way of making their mark through pure action: "Noble six hundred!" They have the capacity for action in an unreasoning world that Eliot's characters all lack, but that the speaker in *Maud* finally achieves:

> Let it flame or fade, and the war roll down like a wind,
> We have proved we have hearts in a cause, we are noble still,
> And myself have awakened, as it seems, to the better mind;
> It is better to fight for the good than to rail at the ill;
> I have felt with my native land, I am one with my kind,
> I embrace the purpose of God, and the doom assigned.
> (III, 54–59)

The connection between action and the mental impulses that occasion it need not be rational for Tennyson. In fact, it cannot be. The succession of lyric and dramatic monologue in *Maud* both shows why it cannot be—humans operate on subjective emotions, that is, the lyric, not the rational—and demonstrates the reality of the human mind. In such a world, it is better to find some channel leading to action than to fall back either on introspection, associated in Tennyson with pure lyric, or on detached, scientific scrutiny of the human condition, associated with the idyll form. Fittingly, Part III, the conclusion of *Maud*, contains no lyric passages and rejects the pastoral idyll:

> No more shall commerce be all in all, and Peace
> Pipe on her pastoral hillock a languid note.   (23–24)

The time has come for Tennyson's own epic action in an unreasoning world. As he approaches *The Idylls of the King*, he too will leave behind peace, piping "on her hillock a languid note."

The Idylls of the King

Whatever his various contemporaries may have felt about Tennyson's *Idylls of the King*—and their opinions differed widely—all were prepared to admit them as the poetic epic of the age. A. E. Housman lamented that through them people would "judge that the Victorian age was an age of milk and water." Gladstone hailed them as epic books on the model of Homer; and W. H. Mallock devised a literary recipe, "How to Make an Epic Poem like Mr. T*NN*-SON":

> Take, then one blameless prig. Set him upright in the middle of a round table, and place beside him a beautiful wife who cannot abide prigs. Add to these one marred goodly man; and tie the three together in a bundle with a link or two of Destiny. Proceed, next, to surround this group with a large number of men and women of the nineteenth century, in fancy-ball costume, flavored with a great many very possible vices, and with a few impossible virtues . . . break the wife's reputation into small pieces; and dust them well over the blameless prig . . . Then wound slightly the head of the blameless prig; remove him suddenly from the table, and keep in a cool barge for future use.[5]

Like Everest, the *Idylls* were indisputably there, evoking both awe and consternation by their ponderous majesty, and they continue today to be both the chief monument of Victorian poetry and the most unapproachable landmark of the period.

One of the central difficulties of *The Idylls of the King* lies in deciding exactly what they are. Gladstone and Mallock identified them as an epic, while Tennyson's own comments stressed their "allegorical or perhaps rather parabolic drift." The poem is indisputably an Arthurian romance on the medieval models, and yet as Mallock points out it is blatantly about "men and woman of the nineteenth century" —Anthony Trollope milked the latter-day parallels in the *Idylls* when he made Lizzie Eustace a devotee of them.[6] They have been denounced for their namby-pamby moralizing (Housman will serve as a spokesman for this view) and reviled as "an incongruous edifice of tradition and invention where even virtue is made to seem either imbecile or vile" (the words are Swinburne's). Though they possess the semblance of a narrative structure, Tennyson nevertheless insisted upon the title *Idylls;* and some critics have stressed their discontinuity, while others have insisted that they possess the unity of drama in their vision and seasonal pattern.[7]

All of these approaches are to some extent borne out by the text of the *Idylls* themselves. Each view contains a portion of the true character of the poem, and the best definition of its form is probably an amalgam of all of them: *The Idylls of the King* are an Arthurian romance composed of twelve idylls so arranged as to form an allegorical, cyclical epic that, while it deals extensively with morals, is itself morally neutral. Because Tennyson had devoted his career to the manipulation of received forms, using the idyll as his primary mode, it is not surprising to find in the crowning poetic achievement of his life, a poem of Homeric scope, the playful, recombinant generic spirit that had been at work in *The Princess, In Memoriam,* and *Maud.* Nor is it surprising that the fusion of so many different forms and traditions at first bewildered the poem's readers. Tennyson's aim, however, was not to bewilder, but to develop the various formal strains of the *Idylls* in such a way that they would mirror the theme of universal process, which is the epic subject of his poem. To see how this takes place it is necessary to examine the poem's generic components.

First, and most obviously, the *Idylls* are just that—idylls. As such, they have continuity with the rest of Tennyson's work: he drew on the tradition of his own poetry for the *Idylls* as freely as he drew upon the classics. Indeed, they may be thought of as a grander reworking of the themes and design of the earlier series of twelve idylls that begins with *The Gardener's Daughter*. Those idylls had moved from a portrait of romantic perfection to the study of the circumstances that undermine the hope of this perfection and corrode the bonds of family, friendship, and society. Each was psychological in focus, concentrating upon the various mental attitudes, leading to the dissolution of social ties, that men adopt in the face of the consequent disappointment. *The Idylls of the King* are a similar study conducted on a similar plan, for the idyll form dictates such a design. By its nature the idyll assumes a psychological approach: its interest lies in the beautiful but dispassionate and objective rendering of different human emotions, often through the isolated voice of some character drawn from earlier poetic tradition. As this was Theocritus' method in his idyll put in the mouth of Homer's Cyclops, so it was Tennyson's when he appropriated Sir Thomas Malory's heroes.

It is helpful in this regard to examine Tennyson's additions to the Arthurian tradition from which he worked. For instance, in *Geraint and Enid*, whose story he adapted very closely from Lady Charlotte Guest's translation of the *Mabinogion*, Tennyson's additions are almost entirely of a psychological character. Whereas the *Mabinogion* merely had Enid riding before Geraint in the section that Tennyson adapted for the opening of his idyll, he inserted an outburst from Geraint designed to bring his state of mind into focus.

> Effeminate as I am,
> I will not fight my way with gilded arms,
> All shall be iron.   (20–22)

He also added lines establishing an interior monologue for Geraint:

For he was ever saying to himself,
"O I that wasted time to tend upon her,
To compass her with sweet observances,
To dress her beautifully and keep her true"—
And there he broke the sentence in his heart
Abruptly.   (38–42)

Tennyson took the shell provided by the Arthurian material and within it constructed the objective psychological studies that are the soul of the idyll. It is precisely this conjunction of romance and overt psychology that many readers find disconcerting. (This is the complaint at the heart of Swinburne's diatribe against the *Idylls*.) When antique heroes are displayed in the mental aspect of the postindustrial age they may seem either pusillanimous or silly. The characters of the original Arthurian legends had been men of resolution and action; in the *Mabinogion*'s story of Geraint and in Chretien de Troyes's *Erec and Enide*, Tennyson's other source for this idyll, the focus is almost entirely upon what the hero does, and the reader is left to infer the mental impetus. Tennyson purposely shifted the accent of his originals in a psychological direction, as the idyll form requires and as he had done in *Maud*.

The result of this shift was that sooner or later all the major characters of the *Idylls* came to be depicted in moments of divided mentality, and the study of these mental states, as they affected the process of choice and action, became a central preoccupation of the poem. Tennyson borrowed one of the earliest lines for his Arthurian epic from Vergil's portrait of epic irresolution, when Aeneas is searching for a way to tell Dido he must leave her: "atque animum nunc huc celerem, nunc dividit illuc." Tennyson rendered it, "This way and that dividing the swift mind" (*Passing of Arthur*, 228), to describe Sir Bedivere's hesitation in throwing Arthur's sword. In Malory, Sir Bedivere does not waver; he simply determines not to do as he has been told. But for Tennyson the psychology of the Arthurian tragedy was the essence of the story, and that psychology largely revolved about weak and indecisive minds. Thus the *Idylls* present a series of portraits of the Arthurian characters, not in the process of action, but in the throes of internal debate. The two major exceptions to this pattern are Arthur and Vivien, neither of whom experiences the mental struggle that marks the rest of the court. Both act without reservation, as befits characters totally assured of and committed to their principles, though their principles are opposites. The rest of the population of Camelot waver. The *Idylls* are not a saga of heroic actions but of the mentality from which action, or inaction, results. The narrative, which had been the decisive feature of the Arthurian romances—and of all primitive romance and epic—was for Tennyson secondary to the psychological drama lying behind the adventure. Hence he said of his Arthurian predecessors, "I could not read through Palmerin of England, nor Amadis of Gaul, or any of those old romances—not even 'Morte d'Arthur,' though with so many fine things in it—But all strung together without Art."[8] The art of the *Idylls* is their psychological structuring, an art for which the idyll, from the Alexandrians forward, had been the form par excellence.

Not that Tennyson ignored or disliked the narrative elements of his story. He took simple delight in narrative. He complained that all the presentation copies he received from authors and publishers were from poets, not novelists, and he longed "to have a novel to read in a million volumes, to last me my life." (Jane Austen was the preferred author for this putative novel.)[9] These were the sentiments of a man who took wholehearted pleasure in narrative. The *Idylls* show this, as *Maud* had; but they also show the inclinations of a man whose favorite novelist was Jane Austen. For the narrative of the *Idylls* is not so much one of actions as it is of attitudes—the only kind of narrative of which the idyll form is capable. That Tennyson moved his plot more in the direction of Jane Austen than of Malory is evident in his handling of the central event of his Arthurian story, the adultery of the Queen and Lancelot.

Malory deals with the adultery very directly—even comically: "And then, as the French book saith, the queen and Launcelot were together. And whether they were abed or at other matters of disports, me list not here of no mention, for love that time was not as is nowadays" (20.3). In Tennyson the adultery is not so much a fact—the reader does not know with any certainty that it has actually occurred until halfway through *Lancelot and Elaine,* when the jealous behavior of the Queen and Lancelot's monologue make it apparent—as it is the psychological crux for the whole of Camelot. Geraint's *accidie*—his failure to participate in life—and his subsequent dolorous adventures with Enid were occasioned "when a rumour rose about the Queen, / Touching her guilty love for Lancelot" (*Marriage of Geraint,* 24–25). Balin's lapse into fratricidal brutishness occurs only after he is persuaded by the gossip that Guinevere's is a "crown-scandalous" (*Balin and Balan,* 384). Balin is totally convinced, as Geraint had been, by *false* rumor: Vivien persuades him that her page has seen Lancelot and Guinevere making love, though Tennyson asserts, "She lied with ease" (518). In other words, the fall of Camelot is not rooted in a deed or fact of any kind, but in the false perceptions of various minds that accept hearsay maliciously related. In all this, Tennyson's interest is not the adultery itself, the actual occurrence of which he is at pains to question, but the reaction of the court to the suspicion of sin. It is the idyllist's preoccupation with attitudes rather than events. Tennyson locates the original lapse of Camelot not in the adultery but in the inability of weak minds either to ascertain the truth or, once understood, to act upon it in an intelligent manner. As in *Walking to the Mail,* he indicates that the root cause of corruption is not so much bad choice or will, but bad thinking and ignorance, which in turn provide the atmosphere in which the manifest evils of the later Idylls can flourish. Though *The Idylls of the King* are often accused of an excessively moral bias, they are, in fact, like classical idyll, a morally neutral examination of attitudes and a dispassionate demonstration of the consequences of these attitudes. They are, like Epicharmus' work, "useful." Tennyson himself was no admirer of moral bias in poetry—he spoke of Baudelaire with apparent disparagement as "a kind of moralist"[10]—and though his Arthurian epic examines how morality works and puts in the mouths of its characters many ethical dicta, the idyll form in which it is couched prevents the work itself from becoming pietistic.

Because the idyll is not content merely to delineate mental and emotional states, it seeks to bring these various states, portrayed in separate idylls, into relations with one another. Theocritus had done this in his first seven idylls, Vergil in his ten eclogues, and Tennyson in his early poetry. By bringing to fruition this epic ambition, latent in the idyll form, Tennyson produced in *The Idylls of the King* a legitimate epic. That he intended to produce a poem in the epic tradition, and that his contemporaries so perceived the *Idylls*, is clear from Gladstone's and Mallock's comments and from Tennyson's composition of the poem. With only the first four Idylls before him, Gladstone had remarked in 1859 that "we would fain have been permitted, at least provisionally, to call these Idylls by the name of Books" in the epic manner.[11] The epic properties became even more manifest as subsequent Idylls appeared: each Idyll was the length of an epic book, and Tennyson was at great pains to bring the total number of books up to the traditional epic number of twelve, a feat he accomplished in exactly the same way that Milton had when he converted *Paradise Lost* from ten books to twelve in order to match the Vergilian proportion. Milton had added his two extra books by simply dividing Book X of the first edition of *Paradise Lost* into three sections and adding five lines. Tennyson likewise took the long idyll, *Enid*, published in 1859, and divided it in 1873 into *The Marriage of Geraint* and *Geraint and Enid*. With the publication of *Balin and Balan* in 1885 (this book had been completed in 1872) the epic number of twelve books was achieved.

But Tennyson's epic union of his twelve idylls is not merely a matter of appearances. He not only imitated the length and number of books in the traditional epic, but followed the process that he considered essential to the creation of a new epic: he "invented his verse." Aubrey de Vere once criticized both Homer's and Milton's epics as containing much that was boring, to which Tennyson replied, "Possibly—but there's the charm of Milton's style. He invented his verse—just as Virgil invented his."[12] Such a goal was clearly in the poet's mind when he approached the *Idylls:* to invent a verse form that was faithful to the tradition of epic and could sustain a narrative of some ten thousand lines while preserving the best elements of his own shorter idylls. The solution came in his distinctive pentameter and his original use of the verse paragraph.

Tennyson had already used the pentameter extensively in poems intended to achieve a wide range of effects. In *Dora* it had served him as a vehicle for sparse, homely narrative, while in *Tithonus* and other monologues it had performed one of the traditional functions of English blank verse, the rendering of dramatic speech. In *The Idylls of the King*, when he had to accommodate simple narrative, speech, and the psychological probing of his earlier idylls within a single form, the pentameter was his natural choice, not only as the traditional meter of the English grand style but as a natural and plastic medium. It is not surprising that much of *The Idylls of the King* is in quotation marks—Tennyson was at home in the monologue form and he had prepared himself for the *Idylls* by writing the monodrama *Maud*. His epic almost seems to be a pastiche of different monologues, something like Browning's *The Ring and the Book*. But through his blank verse and the verse paragraph Tennyson did much more than portray a succession of viewpoints. He picked the most versatile of meters in his stock in order to tie the various dialogues and monologues within the epic into a whole, just as in *Maud* he had used a mixture of anapests and iambs to bring unity to the disparate postures and attitudes of the hero's evolving personality.

Pelleas and Ettarre is a good example of the poet's method. The idyll begins with a straightforward verse paragraph in diction that borders on prose in its narrative simplicity:

> King Arthur made new knights to fill the gap
> Left by the Holy Quest; and as he sat
> In hall at old Caerleon, the high doors
> Were softly sundered, and through these a youth,
> Pelleas, and the sweet smell of the fields
> Past, and the sunshine came along with him.   (1–6)

The simple flow of narrative is reminiscent of Malory's unpretentious prose, but it further establishes the uncomplicated world of perception in which Pelleas moves, for the

hero of the idyll is as yet untainted by the court in which
he has become a knight, unmindful of the paradox when,
on first seeing Ettarre, he says, "fair thou art and pure as
Guinevere" (42). But as the idyll progresses into its description of Gawain's betrayal of Pelleas, the verse and the verse
paragraphs become increasingly complex. At the center of
the idyll, Tennyson incorporates into his unfolding story
a lyric that Pelleas has remembered from the court, "A worm
within the rose":

> A rose, but one, none other rose had I,
> A rose, one rose, and this was wondrous fair,
> One rose, a rose that gladdened earth and sky,
> One rose, my rose, that sweetened all mine air—
> I cared not for the thorns; the thorns were there.
>
> (391–395)

Nowhere is Tennyson's desire to incorporate various
shorter forms into his epic more obvious than in his inclusion
in the *Idylls* of a number of rhymed lyrics among the epic
blank verse, all set in the iambic line surrounding them, but
adding an ominous touch to the idylls in which they appear;
as in *In Memoriam,* Tennyson seems not to have trusted the
lyric form in its pure state. In *Pelleas and Ettarre* the lyric,
like the rose it describes, is a moment of beauty that contains a fatal truth, though the hero is as yet unaware of it.
It is a revealing fact that a large proportion of the lyric
material in *The Idylls of the King* is sung by Vivien. Tennyson wants to associate the sensuous and apparently simple
beauty of the form with the deceptive principle of corruption working to bring down Camelot; and the presence of
such a form forces his poetry to become increasingly stylized
and complicated in order to mirror the world as infiltrated
by the deceptively sweet lyric.

When he has rehearsed the lyric, Pelleas covertly spies on
Gawain and Ettarre and finds them in each other's arms:

> Back, as a hand that pushes through the leaf
> To find a nest and feels a snake, he drew. (417–428)

The simple narrative verse of the opening is now gone, replaced by a poetry of craft and device in which the inversion

of word order mimics Pelleas's recoil and puts the reader into a world of reversed values that can no longer be directly perceived but must be understood at second hand by comparison and simile.

The verse in the rest of the idyll continues to shadow its substance. Pelleas rides off, leaving Gawain and Ettarre asleep,

> And the sword of the tourney across her throat.
>
> And forth he past, and mounted on his horse
> Stared at her towers that, larger than themselves
> In their own darkness, thronged into the moon.
>
> (446–449)

Gerard Manley Hopkins noted that the line, "And the sword of the tourney across her throat" was counterpointed;[13] Tennyson said that it was meant to reproduce the quiver of the sword on flesh, an effect gained by the vowels in combination with the repetition of the trilled *r*'s that force the reader's throat to vibrate as he reads aloud. Extra syllables in this line, and in the line, "Stared at her towers that, larger than themselves," reinforce Pelleas's brutal discovery that the world is out of joint by throwing the poetry out of synchronization, while at the same time imitating Pelleas's engrossed and laboring mind. The idyll concludes with a quick switch from narrative to interior monologue: "And Modred thought, 'The time is hard at hand' " (597). Modred takes advantage of the political chaos in the court caused by the corruption of its members and so the idyll that had begun with simple narrative ends on a complex and dissonant note.

Nor are the epic qualities of the *Idylls* found only in the technical characteristics of its structure. Like Homer, Vergil, and Spenser, Tennyson embarked upon a national, as well as a universal, theme. He followed the trend in epic that evolved after Homer's heroic, social narratives: Vergil had imported from the idyll into the epic (especially in Book IV of the *Aeneid*) an element of romance and an interest in the erotic, emotional Theocritean world that had been foreign to the Homeric epic. Vergil's Italian descendants, Tasso and Ariosto, further exploited this interest in romance, though they were accused in their own time of violating the classical tradition that in fact they were developing. With Milton this romantic aspect of the epic, rooted in the idyllic examination of emotional and mental states, assumed a thoroughly psychological character: *Paradise Lost* is not so much about the Fall as about the psychology leading to it. Wordsworth's *Prelude* takes this psychological dimension of the epic to its logical conclusion in an examination not of some exterior mentality, but of self. Tennyson's epic steps away from Wordsworth's subjectivity (Tennyson's suspicion of the lyric probably hindered him from an epic undertaking on the lines of *The Prelude*), but he fully embraced and expanded upon the clear drift of epic toward romance and psychology, thus fulfilling the demands of both idyll and epic; the concerns of these two forms had become increasingly alike, till in Tennyson they met. (Perhaps this helps to explain the decline of epic in the modern world: as it developed romantic and psychological interests identical to those treated in shorter forms, it put itself out of business.) The *Idylls* are dominated by romance, both in the literary sense in which Tasso's *Gerusalemma liberata* is a romance and in the more modern sense in which the central affair between Lancelot and Guinevere is "romantic."

Tennyson's debt to the Italian tradition of romantic epic, and especially to Tasso, is particularly heavy—though, as with *In Memoriam*, the Italian influence on the *Idylls* has been largely ignored in this century. Tennyson seems to have discovered in Tasso much more than in Spenser how the "allegorical or perhaps rather parabolic drift" of his poem might be achieved. He owned at least three copies of Tasso's romantic epic, two in the original and one in Fairfax's translation.[14] Two of these, the Italian edition of 1728 and the Fairfax translation, are especially interesting, for both contain Tasso's explanation of the allegory of his poem, a summary that is illuminating set side by side with Tennyson's elaboration of the *Idylls*. In Tasso's outline of his allegory, the army besieging Jerusalem represents man as both body and soul, the less noble soldiers being the body while their leader, Godfrey, stands for the "understanding [that] is of God." The goal of their endeavors, Jerusalem, represents the civil happiness of a Christian and is set on a "hill of virtue." The knights surrounding Godfrey, including Rinaldo and Tancred, are the other powers of the soul, and Tancred's destructive love for Clorinda is used as a model of concupiscence defeating reason. In Tennyson's version of the allegory in the *Idylls*, Arthur, on the model of Godfrey, represents "the Ideal in the Soul of Man coming in contact with the warring elements of the flesh." Camelot, like Jerusalem, is a place of civil order founded upon spiritual virtue, while Arthur's knights, like Godfrey's, threaten this balance by their various lapses, Lancelot's failings being most like Tancred's. "The King is the complete man, the Knights are his passions," Tennyson told Allingham in what amounted to a paraphrase of Tasso.[15] Also in Tasso is the canto devoted to Ismen and the enchanted wood, representing "that temptation, which seeketh to deceive with false belief that virtue (as many may call it) opinative"; in Tennyson the wood becomes that of Broceliande and the enchantress Vivien, but the spirit of the allegory remains the same: Vivien deceives Merlin with a false belief that corrupts his judgment. Both Tasso and Tennyson have hermits: Tasso's is designed to show "that the grace of God doth not work always in men immediately, or by extraordinary way, but many times worketh by natural means"—a fair summary of the role played by the simple monk Ambrosius in Tennyson's *Holy Grail*. The parallels between the two systems of allegory are manifold, reminders that Tennyson evolved his poem out of the classical and Renaissance romances and epics, rather than merely producing a Victorian rendition of Malory in Pre-Raphaelite dress.

Of course, the allegory of *The Idylls of the King* is not precisely like that of Tasso. (Knowles said the *Idylls* had an "undertone of symbolism, which, while it never interferes with the clear *melody* of the poem, or perverts it into that most tedious of riddles, a formal allegory, gives a profound harmony to its music".)[16] Tennyson's allegory, which examines universal mental states through single characters, is not quite the same as Tasso's allegory, in which a character represents primarily an abstract virtue or state that may secondarily manifest itself in an emotional condition. Whereas Tasso's Arminda is "that temptation which layeth siege to the power of our desires," Tennyson's Guinevere, besides being a temptation for Lancelot, is a woman who herself is assailed by temptation. Tennyson, by employing the traditions of both the romantic epic and the idyll could give a fuller psychological picture of the world than traditional allegory could by treating its figures solely as idyllic subjects.

The *Idylls* are several things at once. They are an epic on a national theme (the one Milton rejected in favor of the Christian epic), but they are also romance, allegory, and idyll; and to perceive the continuity they achieve demands a recognition of all these strains. For instance, although the *Idylls* have epic scope, it is not the Homeric scope of heroic actions, or even the Vergilian scope of historical destiny, but the psychological scope of the extended idyll. The allegorical elements of the *Idylls* are similarly transformed from their traditional Renaissance usages, and the romantic aspects of the poem do not accent adventure, as it sources do, but anticlimax. The curious amalgam of forms that constitutes the *Idylls*, resulting in a romantic epic of idyllic psychology, demanded a substitution of stasis for action, a necessity that neatly fitted Tennyson's view of his subject matter. The presence of many forms heightens the reader's awareness of the subtle and complex nature of the human condition described in the *Idylls*, and the curious lack of decision demonstrated by their characters reflects the poet's conclusion that a world of various forms might also be a world of deadlock, in which the competing forms held one another back from a transcendent truth.

Precisely because Tennyson was suspicious of the traditional forms even as he used them, he tried to show their range in his new epic but did not wish merely to imitate his models; in part the new genre he created out of traditional material makes fun of the old forms. *Gareth and Lynette* is an allegory against allegory, in which the traditional mode of allegorical identification is mocked by the hero of the piece and by Tennyson himself: "Fool," says Gareth to the allegorical figure of Death,

> Canst thou not trust the limbs thy God hath given,
> But must, to make the terror of them more,
> Trick thyself out in ghastly imageries? (1353–55)

In this early idyll, allegory is finally overthrown and the world stands revealed in the simple freshness of "a blooming boy" (1390). But this natural purity, which is part both of the subject matter of these early idylls and of the more direct, uncomplicated form in which Tennyson expresses the theme, cannot endure in the world of the later idylls. There the "ghastly imageries" Gareth has overthrown return in the plot and also in Tennyson's increasing use of allegorical devices to express the sinuous development of evil in Camelot. According to Tennyson, the forms of poetry must be as complex as the universe it depicts, and if complexity in the world stems from corruption, then poetry must likewise participate in a flawed multiplicity. Similarly, although he employs lyric elements throughout his poem, he shows a deep suspicion of the apparent earnestness and spontaneity of the form—it is Vivien who sings the largest number of lyrics, and in *Merlin and Vivien* she uses them to seduce the magus of the court. The poet would like to have the *Idylls* participate in "that pure severity of perfect light" (*Guinevere*, 641) that Guinevere sees in Arthur and that would radiate from any perfect form; but inasmuch as it describes an imperfect world, it must conform in part to another of Guinevere's maxims: "The low sun makes the colour" (*Lancelot and Elaine*, 134). Because its subject is the flawed mentality of humanity, the poem is necessarily compounded of forms that, taken both individually and as a whole, reflect this condition. But Tennyson reserves the right to manipulate his forms in such a way that what he finds weak or false in them will be exploited to the greater advantage of his theme. Thus he uses allegory, but makes the reader aware, through *Gareth and Lynette*, why he must do so. He uses lyric, but is careful to put the reader on his guard against the form's seeming authenticity by means of the situations in which it is employed. Even the epic form is mocked: traditionally epic is the form of certainty, a description of concrete achievement, but in Tennyson's version all is as uncertain as Arthur's birth, and nonevents, like the abortive Grail quest, are the order of the day. Much of the epic machinery of the *Idylls* is used in furtherance of scenes in which nothing happens, a Tennysonian alteration of the tradition that may baffle readers but that is essential to the poem's design. It throws the reader back upon the internal machinations of the saga, which is Tennyson's first interest, and in addition highlights the incapacity of any form to be ideal in a world that is itself uncertain and confused.

This uncertainty and confusion, a deliberate distortion of the epic inheritance, begins in the first book of the *Idylls*—*The Coming of Arthur*—and is manifest not only in the contradictory versions of Arthur's birth (Malory gives only one version—of the enforced union between Uther and Ygerne) but in Arthur's whole demeanor. Here, as throughout the poem, he is hard to understand and harder still to like. These impressions that the reader is likely to carry away from his first encounter with Arthur are voiced in the text by Guinevere: "She saw him not, or marked not, if she saw, / One among many, though his face was bare" (53–54). Guinevere consistently prefers the more robust Lancelot to Arthur. Even at the end, in the nunnery, "moving through the past unconsciously," she repeats her first impression of Arthur: "High, self-contained, and cold, passionless, not like him, / Not like my Lancelot" (*Guinevere*, 399, 403–405). Her reaction has been echoed by many astute readers: "a prig" is what Mallock called the epic hero. If *The Idylls* were a purely traditional epic, Arthur would indeed be a failure in the role of hero, and the Queen would be correct in assessing Lancelot as the true protagonist, just as Satan would be the true hero of *Paradise Lost* if *Paradise Lost* were a Homeric epic. But the literary forms in which heroes are depicted largely determine their true stature, and in the complex milieu of the *Idylls* Lancelot is no more fit to be a hero than Satan is in Milton's saga. As Milton does with Satan, Tennyson finally puts into Lancelot's mouth a long monologue in which he exposes his own incapacity:

> For what am I? What profits me my name
> Of greatest knight? I fought for it, and have it:
> Pleasure to have it, none; to lose it, pain;
> Now grown a part of me: but what use in it?
> To make men worse by making my sin known?
> > (*Lancelot and Elaine*, 1402–06)

The antiquely heroic Lancelot, the man of physical presence and indefatigable chivalry, is finally reduced to the world of divided mentality that is the milieu of the *Idylls*. In it he fares no better, and perhaps a good deal worse, than his contemporaries. In such a world, where doubt, hesitancy, and indecision arising from inner conflict are the ultimate obstacles, Arthur is the true hero, for he does not suffer from the psychic turmoil born of divided will that surrounds him. This observation may go some way toward defending Arthur from the worst criticism leveled against him: that in his reproach of Guinevere during their last interview in the nunnery he is a self-righteous prig. Arthur's behavior, after all, is a textbook example of the kind of approach twentieth-century psychologists insist is the trademark of mental health: he confronts his problem directly by going to Guinevere; he discharges his anger; and having discharged it he finds room in the cool dispassion left to him to forgive and still to love.

Indeed, Arthur's heroic qualities are a perfect counterpart to the formal qualities Tennyson wished to achieve in the *Idylls*. Arthur, like the form of idyll, is detached, but insightful into the psychology of those around him; yet amid the more traditionally heroic passions and events of the legend, he is the one genuinely epic character. Arthur's posture throughout the *Idylls* is like that of the poet of idylls, overseeing his realm from a distance, and in the framework of the story this comes to bewilder and annoy the larger part of his subjects. But Arthur's posture is only a rendition of Tennyson's own lifelong poetic role as craftsman involved in but detached from his materials, and through Arthur, Tennyson could not only justify his own poetic but proclaim it as a new form of epic vision which, like Arthur's, the world was perhaps not ready to admit.

In *The Holy Grail*, Arthur expounds on the nature of poetic vision as he rebukes Gawain for the supererogation of his quest:

> all the sacred madness of the bard,
> When God made music through them, could but speak
> His music by the framework and the chord.   (873–875)

The visionary, whether he is mystic, poet, or king, is limited by the inherited media through which his vision must be expressed. So Tennyson is limited in what he can say in the

Idylls, just as Arthur is limited in what he can achieve given the flawed human materials out of which Camelot is built. But "eternal process," the guiding spirit of *In Memoriam*, is at work in the *Idylls* as well, and though both king and poet are necessarily subdued to what they work in, there is nevertheless room for advancement even within the tradition that binds them:

> the King must guard
> That which he rules, and is but as the hind
> To whom a space of land is given to plow.
> Who may not wander from the allotted field
> Before his work be done; but, being done,
> Let visions of the night or of the day
> Come, as they will; and many a time they come,
> Until this earth he walks on seems not earth,
> This light that strikes his eyeball is not light,
> This air that smites his forehead is not air
> But vision—yea, his very hand and foot—
> In moments when he feels he cannot die,
> And knows himself no vision to himself,
> Nor the high God a vision, nor that One
> Who rose again: "ye have seen what ye have seen."
>
> (*The Holy Grail*, 901–915)

As it had in *In Memoriam*, the true vision comes only after the traditional forms have been mastered and exhausted. In that poem Tennyson had run through all the accepted forms of elegy and threnody before he was vouchsafed the revelations of Sections XC and CIII. In *The Idylls of the King* true vision comes only to those who, as Arthur says, have patiently worked in the accepted tradition, just as Tennyson had in his structuring of the poem.

In both the *Idylls* and *In Memoriam*, the true vision is the same—a universe shot through and sustained by a divine energy, toward which the material world evolves—and in both the formal structure mirrors the thematic statement of the work. In the *Idylls*, Arthur proclaims himself

> first of all the kings who drew
> The knighthood-errant of this realm and all
> The realm together under me, their Head,
> In that fair order of my Table Round
>
> (*Guinevere*, 457–460)

and Tennyson the patient bard likewise draws together the disparate formal traditions of poetry in a new, unified relation expressing the advance of civilization. The symbol of Arthur's realm, united from separate elements, is his throne, adorned with the dragons, symbolic of his supremacy, which

> Through knots and loops and folds innumerable
> Fled ever through the woodwork, till they found
> The new design wherein they lost themselves,
> Yet with all ease, so tender was the work.
> > (*Lancelot and Elaine*, 437–440)

The craftsmanship figuring forth Arthur's power is duplicated in the intricate melding of traditions that constitutes the *Idylls*, wherein idyll and epic, drama and romance, lyric and allegory are blended so as to lose themselves in a new design partaking of each but surpassing all.

This new poetic medium Tennyson expected to be no better received than Camelot, and of no longer duration, and yet he must have felt it embodied an epic truth that like Arthur and Camelot "will not die / But pass, again to come" (*Coming of Arthur*, 421). This enduring truth is compounded of the totality of human thoughts and feelings groping in their imperfection and ignorance toward newer forms in the eternal process that Tennyson believed not only leads to perfection but already contains it; for the goal of eternal process is but perfect process, and even the present striving toward the goal already embodies in a germinal stage the thing it aims for. In this process, the role of the poet must be the role of King Arthur: the patient and dispassionate craftsman, welding together such diverse and imperfect elements as the time provides, in the knowledge that though the world shaped out of his consciousness and captured in his poetry must pass, it shares in its very transience and diversity the attributes of evolving perfection implanted by the divine poet:

> A various world! which he compelled once more
> Through his own nature, with well mingled hues,
> Into another shape, born of the first,
> As beautiful, but yet another world.[17]

Notes

One. Tennyson and the Uses of Tradition

1. William Allingham, *A Diary*, ed. H. Allingham and D. Dudford (London: Macmillan, 1907), p. 95.

2. Hallam Tennyson, *Alfred Lord Tennyson: A Memoir*, 2 vols. (London, 1897), 2:422–425.

3. The comparison of Vergil and Tennyson is at least as old as Sir Thomas Herbert's parallel treatment of their lives, *Quarterly Review* 193(1901):99–129. G. K. Chesterton's remark that "Tennyson was a provincial Vergil" is meant as a very backhanded compliment; Chesterton uses it to buttress his contention that "Tennyson is the Englishman taking himself seriously—an awful sight." *The Victorian Age in Literature* (New York: Holt, 1913), pp. 162–163. Douglas Bush connects the two poets in "The Personal Note in Tennyson's Classical Poems," *University of Toronto Quarterly* 4(1935):216–217, as does Owen Chadwick in "Tennyson and Vergil," the Tennyson Memorial Sermon, delivered in 1968 and republished in the *Tennyson Research Bulletin* 2(1968), Supplement.

4. Tennyson made this remark to Edmund Gosse, in either 1886 or 1889. For the different versions of the story, see Charles Tennyson, *Alfred Tennyson* (1949; rpt. Hamden, Conn.: Archon Books, 1968), p. 490; and Harold Nicholson, "Tennyson: Fifty Years After," *Poetry Review* 33(1942):334.

5. *Cornhill* 41(1880):36. Collins's Tennyson scholarship is summed up in his *Illustrations of Tennyson* (London, 1891).

6. Alfred Austin, "Tennyson's Literary Sensitiveness," *National Review* 20(1892):454–460.

7. For Tennyson's letter to Wilson clearing himself of any complicity in a pamphlet satirizing Wilson's reviews, see Hallan Tennyson, *Memoir*, 1:93–96. Alfred Austin and John Addington Symonds

both recollected occasions on which Tennyson reminded them, in the friendliest way, of derogatory statements they had made about his work: Austin, "Tennyson's Literary Sensitiveness," p. 458; and Symonds, "Recollections of Tennyson," *Century Magazine*, n.s. 24(1893):36. In both instances, the critic-friends had forgotten the remarks Tennyson remembered so vividly. There are many examples of Tennyson's detestation of Collins. For instance, see Mrs. Montague Butler's "Visit to Farringford," in *Tennyson and His Friends*, ed. Hallam Tennyson (London: Macmillan, 1911), p. 217, where "Z." is Collins; or H. D. Rawnsley, *Memoirs of the Tennysons* (Glasgow, 1900), p. 139, where again Collins is intended.

8. Christopher Ricks's edition, *Poems of Tennyson* (London: Longmans, 1969; New York: Norton, 1972) contains Tennyson's observations on Collins's parallels as notes to the poems Collins referenced. A summary of Tennyson's *Cornhill* marginalia can be found in H. P. Sucksmith, "Tennyson on the Nature of his Own Poetic Genius," *Renaissance and Modern Studies* 11(1967):84–89.

9. *Tennyson and His Friends*, pp. 216–217.

10. Ibid., p. 269; unsigned note in the *Tennyson Research Bulletin* 2(1973):81. Tennyson's remark on Keats and Horace dates from October 18, 1889. For a similar comment ("I never could see I am so like Keats"), see Austin, "Tennyson's Literary Sensitiveness," p. 458.

11. Here and throughout the book, translations are mine unless otherwise noted.

12. *Memoir*, 2:503.

13. Denys Page omits this lyric, fragment 71, from his edition of Sappho (Oxford: Oxford University Press, 1955), but early editors considered it genuine, and Tennyson would have thought it Sapphic.

14. Mrs. Montagu Butler reported of Tennyson that "the discovery for which he always hoped the most was of some further writings of Sappho." *Tennyson and His Friends*, p. 216. For other examples of his use of Sapphic lyrics, see *Memoir*, 1:501; and "Tennyson, Sappho and the Lady of Shalott," *Tennyson Research Bulletin* 2(1975): 171–172. For Hallam's connection of *Mariana in the South* with Sappho, see Hallam Tennyson, *Materials for a Life of Alfred Tennyson*, 4 vols. (privately printed, n.d.), 4:454.

15. An excellent example of criticism that demonstrates not Tennyson's indebtedness to but his manipulation of sources is Paul Turner's "Some Ancient Light on Tennyson's Oenone," *Journal of English and Germanic Philology* (*JEGP*) 61(1962):57–72. Tennyson himself said in a letter (1882) to S. E. Dawson, included in his *Study of "The Princess,"* 2d ed. (Montreal, 1884), p. ix, "It is scarcely possible for anyone to say or write anything at this late time of the world to which, in the rest of the literature of the world, a parallel could not somewhere be found." This is substantially Claudio Guillen's position when he says, "an influence need not assume the recognizable form of a parallelism just as every

parallelism does not proceed from an influence." *Literature as System* (Princeton: Princeton University Press, 1971), p. 35.

16. Ricks's edition separates the two poems; W. D. Paden rightly pointed out that they have a common source in *Measure for Measure*. *Tennyson in Egypt* (1942; rpt. New York: Octagon, 1971), pp. 157n–158n.

Two. The Sources of Tennyson's Idyll

1. Allingham, *Diary*, p. 291.

2. Hallam Tennyson, *Memoir*, 1:508n.

3. Gwenlliam F. Palgrave, *Francis Turner Palgrave, His Journals and Memories of His Life* (London, 1899), p. 64. For evidence of Tennyson's control over the selections in Palgrave's anthology, see B. Ifor Evans, "Tennyson and the Origins of the Golden Treasury," *Times Literary Supplement (TLS)*, December 8, 1932, p. 941.

4. John Churton Collins was one of the first to call Tennyson an Alexandrian, in his *Cornhill* articles, but Edmund Stedman had already pointed out the likeness of the Victorian to the Alexandrian age, and of Tennyson to Theocritus, in his *Victorian Poets* (Boston, 1875). H. Marshall McLuhan restated the similarity, though with emphasis on the mythic and social implications of Theocritean-Tennysonian poetry; see "Tennyson and The Romantic Epic," in *Critical Essays on the Poetry of Tennyson*, ed. John Killham (London: Routledge, 1960), pp. 86–98. In the last few years, Dwight Culler has again emphasized Tennyson's Alexandrian heritage: *The Poetry of Tennyson* (New Haven: Yale University Press, 1977), pp. 90–92.

5. Marjorie Crump puts it nicely: for her, Alexandrian poetry is "characterized by displays of learning and by constant efforts to secure unusual or sensational effects." *The Epyllion from Theocritus to Ovid* (Oxford: Blackwell, 1931), p. 12.

6. The idyll's concern with form, and its habit of calling attention to this concern, are most apparent in the pattern poems of the Hellenistic era, which are in the shapes of the things they describe, such as *The Shepherd's Pipe* or *The Altar*. George Herbert copied the form in his *Altar* and in *Easter-Wings*. In the case of both the Alexandrians and Herbert, the preoccupation with form seems to have been rooted in the Platonic desire to move the reader away from the text to the ideal, which the words only image forth. See the Loeb edition of *The Greek Bucolic Poets* (Cambridge: Harvard University Press, 1960), pp. 487–511, for the ancient pattern poems.

7. Callimachus' famous passage is *Aetia* 1.1.1–6. The text is corrupt—see Rudolph Pfeiffer's two-volume edition (Oxford: Clarendon Press, 1949–1953), 1:1—but the gist is as follows: "The Telchines [here a term of abuse of his literary enemies] who are ignorant and no friends of the muse, murmur against my song, because I have not finished an unbroken poem of thousands of lines

on kings or heroes but tell a little tale, like a child." The important word here is "little," from *tutthon*. Though often translated as "short," *tutthon* is a term applied to children; and the word, coupled with the subsequent reference to childhood, points up Callimachus' meaning: his is to be a young poetry, little because still developing, like a child. He is not saying that the form must always be brief, for the *Aetia* itself is long; he is rather proclaiming that his poetry is newborn and will grow organically to its proper size. The adult form of Callimachus' "little tale" can be seen in Ovid and Vergil.

8. The fragmentation of the idyll and its curiosity about individual psychic states explain the otherwise puzzling recurrence of sorcery as a theme in this form, a recurrence that might have seemed atavistic after the age of Plato and Aristotle. Religion is a unifying social and cultural phenomenon, suitable for epic discussion; its fragmented, individual, self-centered counterpart is magic.

9. Both H. Marshall McLuhan, in his introduction to *Tennyson, Selected Poetry* (New York: Holt, Rinehart, 1956), pp. xiv-xxiv, and J. M. Gray, "Tennyson's Doppelgänger: Balin and Balan," *Bulletin of the Tennyson Research Society* (Lincoln, England, 1971), pp. 3–55, have discussed the discontinuity of the idyll and Tennyson's application of this aspect of the genre. Both emphasize that by avoiding narrative, idyll embraces symbolism and parallelism within its own confines: "Everything becomes symbolic. Linkage and coherence is reached through symbol. By such the poem has an *inner* coherence," says Gray (p. 26). My discussion gives to what Gray and McLuhan call symbolism the more old-fashioned name of allegory. Both authors are right as far as they go; however, the idyll not only seeks inner coherence but aims for epic connections with other idylls and for epic scope.

10. See Gilbert Lawall, *Theocritus' Coan Pastoral* (Cambridge: Harvard University Press, 1967), for a brilliant exposition of the connections between the first seven idylls in Theocritus. Lawall summarizes his study: "Theocritus is all of these figures in the idylls; his characters are not objective portraits drawn from life but are rather symbols of the opposite pulls operative in his own inner self, symbols of his own spiritual world of emotion and fantasy. The subjective impact of the Coan collection is reinforced in the concluding idyll, with its portrait of Theocritus as a newly integrated personality, which inspires and reflects the grand pastoral design of his entire poetry" (p. 13). I would argue with this formulation only in its ascribing the various emotional states portrayed in the idylls to Theocritus personally: are they not depictions of universal states, and if so, why particularize them to the author? All translations of Theocritus in this work, except those of the lines from Idylls II and V, are from A. S. F. Gow's two-volume *Theocritus*, 2d ed. (Cambridge: Cambridge University Press, 1965).

11. The history of the dramatic monologue has been variously deduced by different authors. Mungo W. MacCallum's "The Dra-

matic Monologue in the Victorian Period," *Proceedings of the British Academy, 1924–1925,* pp. 265–282, which examines only the British antecedents of the form, finds early examples in Drayton and Daniel, but not, curiously, in Chaucer's prologue to the Wife of Bath's tale. His observation that the author of monologues "is able to ransack all the recesses and galleries of man's nature and penetrate to its most sacred or opprobrious shrines" applies equally to all the poetry that I term idyll. Ina Beth Sessions, in "The Dramatic Monologue," *PMLA* 52(1947):503–537, divides the genre into so many subgenres (perfect, formal, approximate, etc.) that the reader is likely to lose his grasp on what monologues have in common with one another and with the other poetry that collectively makes up idyll. Robert Langbaum's *The Poetry of Experience: The Dramatic Monologue in Modern Literary Tradition* (London: Chatto and Windus, 1957), treats the monologue, wrongly, as a form brought to full development only in the nineteenth century, and primarily by Browning; he finds a heritage for the form no earlier than the seventeenth century. K. E. Fass, in "Notes towards a History of the Dramatic Monologue," *Anglia* 88(1970):222–232, also argues that the genre was "first established as a tradition by Browning and Tennyson" (p. 223), though he charts its history as far back as Pope's *Dying Christian* (1730). The best treatment of the monologue's history is A. Dwight Culler's "Monodrama and the Dramatic Monologue," *PMLA* 90(1975):366–385, which properly places the form in the tradition of Ovid's *Heroides.* Ovid, however, was imitating the Alexandrians, who in turn had taken the concept from the pastoral mimes of Sophron and Epicharmus, as well as from the soliloquies of the Greek drama. The dramatic monologue really does have dramatic antecedents.

12. In his second edition of Theocritus, A. S. F. Gow says (1:lxxiii) "Theocritus' dialect is artificial, peculiar to himself, and not consistent even in his own usage . . . To write in Doric at all was something of a mannerism or conscious rusticity."

13. See H. Montagu Butler, "Recollections of Tennyson," in *Tennyson and His Friends,* p. 213, for Tennyson's preference for the Greek meters.

14. A fine exposition of the artificiality of Propertius' elegies and their underlying thematic connections is Steele Commager's *A Prolegomenon to Propertius* (Norman: University of Oklahoma Press, 1974). Commager's book and Lawall's *Coan Pastoral* offer an introduction to the sort of linkage that regularly occurred in shorter poetry of the Hellenistic period and after.

15. See Brooks Otis, *Ovid as an Epic Poet,* 2d ed. (Cambridge: Cambridge University Press, 1970), for a full treatment of this subject.

16. Note that in Ovid's opening lines to the *Metamorphoses* (1.1–2), "In nova fert animus mutatas dicere formas/corpora" ("The spirit turns to relate how forms have changed into new

bodies"), he not only announces the subject of his volume but proclaims a literary theory of formal evolution as well, for the *Metamorphoses* is nothing if not a form changing to a new body.

17. Two of the several copies of Vergil that Tennyson owned and that are now in the Tennyson library at Lincoln contain Servius' commentaries: *Bucolica et Georgica* (London, 1774), and the complete works (Amsterdam, 1746). Tennyson placed his initials in both these volumes, usually a sign of his interest in a particular volume or edition. Like the Renaissance poets, Tennyson was familiar with the allegorical possibilities in Vergil.

Whenever this study mentions books in Tennyson's library, the information, unless otherwise noted, is derived from *Tennyson in Lincoln: A Catalogue of the Collections in the Research Centre*, comp. Nancie Campbell, 2 vols. (Tennyson Research Society: Lincoln, 1971, 1973). The second volume lists alphabetically by author all the works in the Tennyson Research Centre that came from Tennyson's, Hallam Tennyson's, Charles Turner-Tennyson's, or the Sellwood family's libraries. Thus it is not a record of everything Tennyson owned, but only of what has survived.

18. If the development of Roman satire was independent of the Hellenistic development of the idyll, it was at least parallel. Satire, from *satura*, grew out of the satyr plays of the Italian countryside just as the idyll, in one manifestation, developed from Greek mime. T. E. Wright, however, speaks of "the principle of *contaminatio* which is so characteristic of Roman poetry as a whole"; and it is likely that satire, as well as all the other Roman forms, partook of this *contaminatio*, or melding with the Greek tradition. *Fifty Years (and Twelve) of Classical Scholarship*, ed. Maurice Platnauer, 2d ed. (New York: Barnes and Noble, 1968), p. 410.

19. Alan Armstrong's "The Apprenticeship of John Donne: Ovid and the Elegies," *JEGP* 76(1977):419–442, discusses in detail Donne's debt to Ovid and the elegiac tradition, from which Donne extracted the "persona's continual self-conscious playing upon that conventional elegiac in modes which keep its artifice in the foreground" (431). Armstrong has isolated several elements in both Ovid and Donne that properly belong to the whole idyllic tradition.

20. *The Letters of William and Dorothy Wordsworth*, ed. Ernest de Selincourt, 2d ed. (Oxford: Clarendon Press, 1967), 1:314–315.

Three. Tennyson's Early Poetry and the Idyllic Tradition

1. "I soon found if I mean to make any mark at all it must be by shortness, for all the men before me had been so diffuse, and all the big things had been done," Tennyson told James Knowles late in life. "Aspects of Tennyson," part 2, *Nineteenth Century* 33 (January 1893):173. The choice for brevity had also been made by the Alexandrians in the face of Homer. Like Callimachus, who championed the short form over the long, Tennyson went on to write very long poems indeed.

2. Allingham, *Diary*, p. 302.

3. Ricks's edition of Tennyson, probably the most thorough treatment of any Victorian author so far undertaken, places the poems as nearly as possible in their order of composition, though as Ricks points out (p. xxii), this arrangement obscures Tennyson's own marshaling of the poems. I am more interested in how Tennyson fitted the poems together than in their chronology, and consequently I have drawn on the Ricks edition for the text of the poems but on the various editions published during Tennyson's lifetime for their order. Renato Poggioli says that "unwritten poetics have existed in every age," and that "modern poetics . . . is generally unwritten." "Poetics and Metrics," in *Proceedings of the Second Congress of the International Comparative Literature Association*, ed. Werner P. Friederick (Chapel Hill, N.C., 1959), pp. 345–346. No better exemplar of this dictum exists than Tennyson, in the Victorian age, for although he clearly possessed an acute critical sense, especially toward formal questions, he left no critical statement of any sort; and his conversational forays should not be given a weight they do not deserve. Victorian England generally was not keen to put into writing its theory of poetics. Pathetically, apart from Matthew Arnold's criticism, the foremost work of the age strictly on the subject of poetics is E. S. Dallas's *The Gay Science* (London, 1866), a dreary, pseudoscientific exposition of genres and modes of poetry. In the absence of an explicit Victorian poetic, conclusions as to what the age believed must be interpolated from the texts and other evidence.

4. *Athenaeum* 91 (1829):456. For Tennyson's editing of his early work, see Joyce Green, "Tennyson's Development during the 'Ten Years' Silence,'" *PMLA* 66(1951):662–697; and Edgar F. Shannon, Jr., *Tennyson and the Reviewers* (Cambridge: Harvard University Press, 1952). Both point out that Tennyson enjoyed early critical esteem, that he dealt objectively with his critics, and most important, that he revised his poetry primarily in accord with his own artistic principles, not in morbid response to reviewers.

5. As an example of the disappearance of "darling" from Tennyson's verse, see *The Miller's Daughter*, 17–23, where "My darling Alice, we must die," becomes after 1832, "My own sweet Alice, we must die."

6. For Tennyson's early experiments in stanza and meter, see James Francis Pyre, *The Formation of Tennyson's Style* (Madison: University of Wisconsin Press, 1921).

7. For the origins of *The Lady of Shalott*, see Paden, *Tennyson in Egypt*, pp. 155n–156n, and D. Laurence Chambers, "Tennysonia," *Modern Language Notes* 18(1903):227–233.

8. *Materials for a Life of Alfred Tennyson*, 4:461. In this discussion, I have used the term "allegory" rather than the more modern "symbolism" because I believe it is clearer and closer to the tradition in which Tennyson was operating.

9. *The Writings of Arthur Hallam,* ed. T. H. Vail Motter (New York: Modern Language Association, 1943), p. 197.

10. Compare, for instance, the *a a a a b c c c b* rhyme scheme and the meter of *The Lady of Shalott* with the following verse from Scott's *Lord of the Isles:*

> She watch'd, yet fear'd to meet his glance,
> And he shunn'd hers; till when by chance
> They met, the point of foreman's lance
>   Had given a milder pang!
> Beneath the intolerable smart
> He writhed, then sternly mann'd his heart
> To play his hard but destined part,
>   And from the table sprang.   (2.55.1–8)

Tennyson simply added an extra line to the first series of rhymed lines.

11. For the Jungian interpretation of the Lady and other Tennysonian females, see Lionel Stevenson, "The 'High-Born Maiden' Symbol in Tennyson," in *Critical Essays on the Poetry of Tennyson,* pp. 126–136; for the Freudian interpretation, see Clyde Ryals, "The 'Fatal Woman' Symbol in Tennyson," *PMLA* 74(1959):438–443.

12. Douglas Bush says of Tennyson's Athena in *Oenone* that she is "so very Victorian that we become embarrassingly aware that she is undressed, apart from a spear, and it seems as if the Queen herself had started up in her bath and begun to address the Duke of Argyll." *Mythology and the Romantic Tradition in English Poetry* (Cambridge: Harvard University Press, 1937), p. 205. Queen Victoria was not on the throne when *Oenone* was published in 1832; the poem is thoroughly eighteenth-century in its classical detail.

13. The dramatic-monologue format of *The Hesperides,* which James D. Merriam points out in "The Poet as Heroic Thief," *Victorian Newsletter* 35(1969):1–5, badly damages G. Robert Stange's argument that the poem is a statement of Tennyson's own artistic beliefs. "Tennyson's Garden of Art," in *Critical Essays on the Poetry of Tennyson,* pp. 99–112. It may be a statement of someone's artistic credo, but it is definitely not Tennyson's: the dreamy melancholy of the sisters' song no more represents Tennyson's own robust and playful sense of poetics than the voice of despair in *The Two Voices* states his view of life.

14. See Ricks, *Poems,* p. 541n.

15. William Cadbury, in what is probably the best article to date on *The Palace of Art,* "Tennyson's 'Palace of Art' and the Rhetoric of Structures," *Criticism* 7(1965):23–44, points out, in opposition to Lionel Stevenson, that " 'The Palace of Art' is not dramatic monologue, but that this is so does not make it literal confession"

(p. 25n). He treats the poem as a study of the psyche reaching for integration and finding the means toward this end in the pastoral imagery of the final lines. *The Palace of Art,* if it is not dramatic monologue, is extremely close to it. Elizabeth Barrett Browning was early dismayed by Tennyson's trick of always speaking through a character, never in propria persona: "Tennyson seldom uses the *ego* of poet-dom; and when he does you generally find that he does not refer to himself, but to some imaginary person. He permits the reader to behold the workings of his individuality, only by a reflex action . . . We know nothing of him except that he is a poet; and this, although it is something, to be sure, does not help us to pronounce distinctly upon what may be called the mental intention of his poetry." Quoted in *Literary Anecdotes of the Nineteenth Century,* ed. W. Robertson Nicoll and Thomas J. Wise (London, 1895), 1:39. Indeed, the "reflex action" of Tennyson's poetry is an excellent description of the idyll's distance and artificiality.

16. Tennyson moved these lines from their position in the middle of the Soul's proud assessment of art to the end, in order that they might summarize her views. See Ricks, *Poems,* pp. 409n, 414n.

17. John Henry Newman, *Apologia pro Vita Sua* (Boston: Houghton Mfflin, 1956), p. 25.

18. "It is necessary to respect the limits," Tennyson told James Knowles. "An artist is one who recognizes bounds to his work as a necessity, and does not overflow illimitably to all extent about a matter." "Aspects of Tennyson," p. 173. The Soul of *The Palace of Art,* in failing to live out this definition, ruins herself and must be restored by a retreat to the milieu of the most disciplined of forms, the pastoral idyll.

Four. The English Idyls and Other Poems

1. Leigh Hunt objected to "such exordiums" as introductions to larger works: "This kind of mixed tone of contempt and non-chalance, or at best, of fine-life phrases with better fellowship, looks a little instructive, and is, at all events, a little perilous." *Church of England Quarterly Review* (October 1842), quoted in Ricks, *Poems,* p. 732. This is one criticism to which Tennyson did not respond by amending—and how could he? The framing device is the soul of the idyll, and it was more important to create the artistic distance than to save the poems from preciousness.

2. The seasonal pattern of *The Idylls of the King* has been much studied; see, for instance, Henry Kozicki's "Tennyson's *Idylls of the King* as Tragic Drama," *Victorian Poetry,* 4(1966), 15–20; and John Rosenberg's *The Fall of Camelot: A Study of Tennyson's Idylls of the King* (Cambridge: Harvard University Press, 1973), p. 28. This series of idylls likewise has a seasonal cycle: it begins in the spring and ends in the fall, if I am right in thinking that the

speaker of *Locksley Hall*, in mentioning the bugle-horn in the poem's first stanza, indicates the autumn hunting seasons as the time frame of the idyll.

3. A number of the idylls in this series feature large buildings that dominate the landscape: Audley Court, Sir Edward's manor house in *Walking to the Mail;* the Hills's estate in *Edwin Morris;* the manor house on whose grounds the Talking Oak flourishes; and of course, Locksley Hall. In this, Tennyson's idyll of the perfect state, the large building is a church. (We hear nothing of the estate on which the gardener's daughter works.) By implication, the introduction of secular structures opens the way to a host of social challenges to the garden state. But the secular estate—and the challenges—are purposely absent from *The Gardener's Daughter,* where perfection is the keynote.

4. In his edition of Tennyson, Ricks (p. 510) attributes the "murmurous wings" to Keats's influence: "The murmurous haunt of flies on summer eves," *Ode to a Nightingale,* 50. Much more likely as a source is Vergil's often repeated, and often onomatopoeic interest in bees—bees being appropriate in Tennyson's poem because of their association with romance and reproduction; see *Eclogues* 2.55 and 7.13. It is more fitting, of course, that Tennyson echo Vergil in the English Idyls, his equivalent of the *Eclogues,* than that he reproduce Keats.

5. The full title of the poem, *The Gardener's Daughter; or, The Pictures,* plays on both the profession of the narrator and the idyll form itself. The poem is a picture about a picture. The title is good evidence that Tennyson believed *eidyllion,* the Greek word for idyll, to have the root meaning of "little picture," a conjecture about which there is some controversy; see J. M. Edmonds's introduction in his Loeb edition of *The Greek Bucolic Poets* (Cambridge: Harvard University Press, 1960), p. xx.

6. If *The Gardener's Daughter* lacks admirers today, it did not at its publication. The Duke of Argyll wrote in his memoirs of a day in his youth spent hunting in solitude on Ben More: "There was present to me that day an internal landscape—not the present or past, but of the future—into which I gazed with the joy of great hopes . . . All poetry I knew fell short of expressing what I felt that day of my delight—all—until, in later years, I read for the first time certain lines [the lines just quoted] of him who soon became the sole master of my poetic fancy." *Autobiography* (New York: E. P. Dutton, 1906), 1:63–68. Note that the Duke immediately sensed Tennyson's poetry as the analogue to "an internal landscape."

7. J. H. Buckley speaks of the "simple assertive sentences intended perhaps to achieve the elemental effect of a Biblical parable." *Tennyson* (Boston: Houghton Mifflin, 1960), p. 80.

8. Tennyson makes a further link between the poems in this series by employing a set of names that vary only slightly. The characters in *Audley Court* are Francis Hale, Edward Head, Letty Hill; in

The Epic, the names are Francis Allen, and Everard Hall; Allan, though spelled differently, is also the name of the farmer in *Dora*. Perhaps Tennyson's inventive powers failed him when it came to naming his characters, but more likely he was seeking to establish a small fund of interchangeable names on the models of Daphnis, Lycidas, and Damon.

9. *Edwin Morris* is generally read as a thinly veiled allegory of Tennyson's romantic failure with Rosa Baring; see the Ricks edition, p. 708. This type of biographical reading constantly befuddles Tennyson criticism. It would interfere with the perception of larger patterns at work in this series of poems by making one poem (*Edwin Morris*, for instance) a sort of confession and another (*The Gardener's Daughter* perhaps) a pastoral romance presumably detached from Tennyson's own experience. This approach ignores the essential similarity of the two poems and the craftsmanship (as opposed to mere self-revelation) that went into producing the contrast.

10. *The Decline and Fall of the Roman Empire* (London: Dent, 1974), 4:18 (ch. 37).

11. Ibid. Tennyson was enough of an admirer of Chaucer to include him in the poetic pantheon of names engraved over his fireplace at Aldworth (The others were Shakespeare, Milton, Wordsworth, Dante, and Goethe.) Why, then, does Derek Brewer say of Chaucer, "all our greatest poets but Tennyson encourage us to believe that here is great poetry"? *Geoffrey Chaucer*, ed. Brewer (Athens: University of Ohio Press, 1975), p. 8.

12. The lyrical stanza of *The Talking Oak* is not a barrier to its being an idyll; after all, *Will Waterproof's Lyrical Monologue*, written at the same time as *The Talking Oak* (1837–38?), reveals in its title Tennyson's interest in experimenting with the lyrical possibilities of the idyll form. In its setting, its recapitulation of English history, and its overall humor, *The Talking Oak* is reminiscent of Marvell's *Upon Appleton House*.

13. Once again, damage has been done by treating this poem as a purely autobiographical, and therefore lyrical, statement by Tennyson on his broken engagement with Emily Sellwood. Like the other poems that seem to imitate Tennyson's life, it may have a biographical source, but the poet himself was at pains to place it in a more objective context. Tennyson seems to have wanted *Love and Duty* to be read as a dramatic monologue, and he looked for "a historical foundation" on which to base it: "I would have it put into the mouth of some noted man . . . involved in . . . a marriage which he does not like, in violation of a pre-existing attachment." *Tennyson and His Friends*, p. 408. It is not odd that such a complicated set of preconditions could not be met by any one historical incident, and the poem was published without its framing device; but in spirit *Love and Duty* belongs with *Ulysses* and *Tithonus* as a monologue.

14. *Memoir*, 1:459.
15. Ibid, p. 195.

Five. *The Fuller Minstrel*

1. T. S. Eliot, *Selected Essays* (New York: Harcourt, Brace, 1964), p. 289. Many critics have remarked on the idyllic nature of *The Princess;* a useful summary of this criticism is found in Henry Kozicki's "The 'Medieval Ideal' in Tennyson's 'The Princess,'" *Criticism* 17(1975):130. More recently, *The Princess* has been called the first effort among Tennyson's later "comic strategies." James Kincaid, *Tennyson's Major Poems* (New Haven: Yale University Press, 1975), p. 3. Dwight Culler reaches a similar conclusion when he says that the Prince, in proposing to the Princess, "was essentially asking her to take up her abode in the English Idyl. For this form, based on love, centering upon marriage and the child, is that which [Tennyson] found most in harmony with his genius. Certainly it is that in which his poetic problems were ultimately resolved." *Tennyson*, p. 148. These observations seem to me only part of the truth. *The Princess* is idyllic, but it is idyll seeking to break out of the mold. Insofar as it is idyllic, it is playful and comic; but it would be a mistake to call this, the first of Tennyson's attempts beyond pure idyll, the form "in which his poetic problems were ultimately resolved," just as it would be to equate the man and the ape because they share certain evolutionary features.

2. Jerome Buckley discusses the mock epic features of *The Princess* in *Tennyson*, pp. 97–98. On the poem as medley, see John Killham, *Tennyson and The Princess: Reflections of an Age* (London: Athlone Press, 1958), pp. 4–5, 275. Killham believes that Tennyson evolved the "medley" form of *The Princess* to produce a genre "capable of representing the singular diversity of his time" (p. 4).

3. Hallam Tennyson, relating his father's sentiments on *The Princess*, in *Memoir*, 1:25.

4. John Killham, "Tennyson's *Maud:* The Function of the Imagery," in *Critical Essays on Tennyson*, pp. 229–230, says that the lines

"Are you that Psyche," Florian asked, "to whom,
In gentler days, your arrow-wounded fawn
Came flying while you sat beside the well?" (II, 251–253)

refer the reader to Marvell's *Nymph Complaining for the Death of Her Fawn*. If this is accurate—and beyond doubt it is—it is another proof of the care with which Tennyson employed allusions. In Marvell's poem the nymph's ending wish is to turn into a statue, as Psyche and the other ladies of Ida's college do.

5. Tennyson to Frederick Locker-Lampson, in *Memoir*, 2:71.

6. Leavis, "Thought and Emotional Quality: Notes in the Analysis of Poetry," *Scrutiny* 13(1945):59.

7. T. S. Eliot, *Selected Essays*, p. 291.

8. See *Memoir*, 1:282. W. D. Paden, in "A Note on the Variants of *In Memoriam* and 'Lucretius,'" *The Library* 8(1953):259–273, dates the letter to November 1849. Fitzgerald's letter to W. B. Dunne is in his *Letters and Literary Remains* (London, 1889), 1:149, where *In Memoriam* is described as "the autobiography of a mourner" (p. 139).

9. Hermann Frankel, *Early Greek Poetry and Philosophy*, trans. Moses Hadas and James Willis (1962; New York: Harcourt Brace Jovanovich, 1975), p. 152.

10. *Memoir*, 1:304. James Knowles, "Aspects of Tennyson," p. 185; the stanza in question was XCIV, 9–12. A. C. Bradley, *A Commentary on In Memoriam*, 3d ed. (London: Macmillan, 1910), is still the best study of the continuity and structure of the poem. It should, however, be read in tandem with Tennyson's remarks to James Knowles in "Aspects of Tennyson," and several more recent works on its organization. Of these recent works see especially E. D. H. Johnson, "In Memoriam: The Way of the Poet," *Victorian Studies* 2(1958):139–148, where the poem is viewed as a search not only for faith but for a formal equivalent of faith (unfortunately this idea is not well developed in the article); and Alan Sinfield's study, *The Language of Tennyson's In Memoriam* (New York: Barnes and Noble, 1971), which treats the structure and language of the poem as "the product of a desperate need for order in the absence of any clear and agreed means of establishing it" (p. 39). Andrew Fichter's "Ode and Elegy: Idea and Form in Tennyson's Early Poetry," *English Literary History (ELH)* 40(1973):398–427, also addresses itself to the form of *In Memoriam*, concluding: "If Tennyson felt a disparity between his thought and the poetic traditions [of the Romantics] he inherited, it is because he treats existential discontinuities as problems of knowledge rather than aspects of poetic form" (p. 399). This conclusion seems unfair to the dazzling formal process of *In Memoriam*, especially in light of Fichter's own correct observation that "the elegiac conventions themselves paradoxically become the subject of *In Memoriam*" (p. 421), and Tennyson's ironic blast at "high wisdom" (CXII) as a means of approaching form.

11. The review that treated *In Memoriam* as "from a female hand" appeared in the *Literary Gazette*, June 15, 1850, p. 407. Tennyson's comment about the scope of the poem is reported by Knowles, "Aspects of Tennyson," p. 182.

12. "*In Memoriam* is a Platonic poem about love," wrote Martin J. Svaglic, in "A Framework for Tennyson's *In Memoriam*," *JEGP* 6(1962):812. About love, yes, but Platonic? Tennyson did not much care for Plato—"Tennyson says he has not really got anything from him," observed Allingham (*Diary*, p. 148)—probably because of the Platonic notion of matter and time as unreal. If Tennyson had accepted this premise, there would have been no need for *In Memoriam*.

13. See, for instance, Harold Bloom, *The Ringers of the Tower* (Chicago: Chicago University Press, 1971), where *In Memoriam* is used as a foil for the glorification of *Adonais*, revealing Shelley's poem as "an attempt to make the elegy a vehicle for not less than everything a particular poet has to say on the ultimates of human existence. Yet Tennyson, for all his ambition, stays within the bounds of elegy" (p. 110). In fact, *Adonais* is much more tradition-bound than *In Memoriam*, as suits Shelley's belief that beneath the apparent flux of the universe there exists an unyielding unity, which *Adonais* imitates in its unity with traditional Greek form. Tennyson had no such notion, and his lyric becomes part of the flux, which he considers quite real.

14. See *Memoir*, 1:162, 223.

15. Charles Tennyson, *Tennyson*, pp. 249–250.

16. *Writings of Arthur Hallam*, p. 197.

17. A. W. Schlegel, *A Course of Lectures on Dramatic Art and Literature*, trans. John Black, rev. ed. (London, 1846), p. 50. Victor Hugo, *Cromwell* (Paris, n.d.), pp. 7, 9.

18. *Writings of Arthur Hallam*, p. 234.

19. Tennyson was an admirer of Hugo and wrote a sonnet on him, though "he reminds one that there is only a small step between the sublime and the ridiculous" (*Memoir*, 2:422). Tennyson's library contained numerous volumes by Hugo (loving novels, the bard would especially have appreciated the epic narratives), and his own historical dramas suggest that he was familiar with Hugo's *Cromwell*. Tennyson would undoubtedly have disputed Hugo's elevation of the grotesque as a vital part of Christian literary evolution: *In Memoriam* is melancholy, but never grotesque. If anyone doubts that *In Memoriam* shares the *ésprit mélancolique* of French Romanticism as represented by Hugo and Chateaubriand, let him compare the beautiful Tennysonian lines (CXVI, 1–4),

> Is it, then, regret for buried time
> That keenlier in sweet April wakes,
> And meets the year, and gives and takes
> The colors of the crescent prime?

with Chateaubriand's similar emotions: "Ce qui enchante dans l'âge des liaisons devient dans l'âge délaissé un objet de souffrance et de regrets. On ne souhaite plus le retour des moins riants à la terre; on le craint plutôt: les oiseaux, les fleurs, une belle soirée de la fin d'avril, une belle nuit commencée le soir avec le premier rossignol, achevée le matin avec la première hirondelle, ces choses qui donnent le besoin et le désir du bonheur, vous tuent." *Memoires de l'outre-tombe*, ed. Maurice Levaillant and Georges Mouliner 3d ed. (Paris: Gallimard, 1957), 1:349(1.10.3).

It is not certain that Tennyson read German critical theory, though Schlegel was available in his circle at the time he was writing *In Memoriam.* Fitzgerald wrote to Tennyson's brother Frederick in October 1841, "Reading Schlegel's lectures on the History of Literature: a nice book." *Letters* (London, 1907), 1:92. Tennyson himself read a good deal of German immediately after Hallam's death, judging by his daily schedule; *Memoir,* 1:124.

20. *Writings of Arthur Hallam,* p. 223.

21. "Tennyson's admiration for Dante might almost be inferred from the fact of his intimacy with Arthur Henry Hallam, for it is well known that Hallam's veneration for Dante amounted almost to a religion." Albert S. Cook, "The Literary Genealogy of Tennyson's *Ulysses,*" *Poet-Lore* 3(1891):499. In one of the few instances for which Ricks's edition of Tennyson can be faulted, its notes to *Ulysses* (p. 560) give the impression that Tennyson relied upon Cary's translation for his knowledge of Dante. In fact, Tennyson owned at least eleven copies of Dante, and the one bearing the inscription "A.T., favorite Dante," is in the original language: *Divina Commedia* (Paris, 1818–19). To underestimate Tennyson's knowledge of Italian is to fail to see his important relation to the formal theory of the continental Renaissance. For Tennyson's early knowledge of Italian, see *Memoir,* 1:7–8. Precisely when Tennyson learned Italian is a matter of conjecture, but he himself gave an amusing description of the process to Allingham (*Diary,* p. 303). Italian seems to have been a common accomplishment among Tennyson's Lincolnshire set; his future bride, Emily Sellwood, read Ariosto and Tasso when she was eighteen (*Tennyson and His Friends,* p. 6), and on as important an occasion as her twenty-first birthday her father gave her a two-volume Italian edition of Tasso's *Gerusalemme e l'Aminta.* When Hallam "lay and read/ The Tuscan poets on the lawn," (LXXXIX, 23–24), he did so in the original, and his audience understood him. Tennyson's comparison of *In Memoriam* and *The Divine Comedy* is in Knowles, "Aspects of Tennyson," p. 182.

22. John Churton Collins, in his fashion of citing parallels shotgun style, found many references to the literature of the Italian Renaissance in *In Memoriam.* See his edition of *In Memoriam, The Princess, and Maud* (London, Methuen, 1902); and his *Cornhill* article (January 1880), pp. 37–38.

23. The book in question is volume four of Dante's *Divina Commedia* (London, 1808–09), containing only the canzone and sonnets, with the markings "A. H. Hallam 1828" and "Alfred Tennyson" in Hallam's hand. The volumes containing the *Commedia* itself have no such markings.

24. These lines were surely the source for Nabokov's lines in *Pale Fire:*

> I was the shadow of the waxwing slain
> By the false azure in the windowpane.   (I, 1–2)

The whole of that novel, as of Nabokov's conception of English poetry, was tempered by his reading of *In Memoriam*. See his "Notes on Prosody," an appendix to his commentary on his translation of *Eugene Onegin*, 4 vols. (London: Routledge & Kegan Paul, 1964), 3:448–540, in which he uses *In Memoriam* ("by far [Tennyson's] best work," p. 460) almost exclusively to exemplify English iambics. In my view *In Memoriam* is probably not the best example of English iambics, since meter, as Schopenhauer observed, "as mere rhythm, has its existence only in time." *The World as Will and Idea*, trans. R. B. Haldane and J. Kemp, 3d ed. (Boston, 1886), 3:205. For this reason, meter is one of the first elements that Tennyson would have regulated in a poem given over to a discussion of time. In fact, the iambics of *In Memoriam*, with its diction, are almost noiseless and seamless, creating in their uninterrupted and even flow exactly the crystalline image of cohesive flux toward perfection that the poem finally embraces. But Nabokov's perceptions about the meter of *In Memoriam*, if not valid for all English poetry, are the best thing on the subject since Saintsbury's *History of English Prosody*, 2d ed. (1923; rpt. New York: Russell and Russell, 1961), 3:203–206.

25. John Rosenberg, "The Two Kingdoms of *In Memoriam*," *JEGP* 58(1959), adduces all of the pastoral sections of the poem and says of them, "Despite Tennyson's personalization of the traditional elegy, he was too resourceful not to use its conventions to mute the louder notes of his anguish" (p. 232n). This is surely correct. It might be supplemented by saying that the pastoral is present not only to mute the tone but as an integral part of the poem's development, though I cannot agree with F. E. L. Priestley, who contends that the core of *In Memoriam* is "the traditional classical elegiac form." *Language and Structure in Tennyson's Poetry* (London: André Deutsch, 1973), p. 120. The point about *In Memoriam* is that it outgrows pastoral elegy.

26. The phrase "eternal process" was especially favored by Tennyson; he used it to summarize Alfred Wallace's philosophy of matter and time, of which he approved: "Wallace says the system he believes in is a far finer one than Christianity; it is eternal process—I have always felt there must be somewhere *Some one who knows*, that is, *God*." Allingham, *Diary*, p. 339.

27. These lines are usually glossed, from Tennyson's own notes, as a reference to Goethe's philosophy, and the date of their composition assigned after 1846. Hallam Tennyson's *Material for a Life of Alfred Tennyson*, 2:183, however, gives them as an early section; and a recently published letter of Tennyson's to Emily Sellwood, written probably in the fall of 1839, uses similar phrasing: "Thou hast proven time and space very prettily. So mayest thou and I and all of us ascend stepwise to Perfection." James O. Hoge, "Tennyson and Emily Sellwood: Unpublished Letter Fragments," *Tennyson Research Society Bulletin* 2, no. 2(1972):56.

28. Whitehead, *Process and Reality*, new ed. (New York: Free Press, 1978), p. 104. *In Memoriam* might be said to be a poetic rendition of the philosophy of organism, though Whitehead felt Tennyson's orientation toward "one far-off divine event" was not congenial to his own thought (p. 111). Nevertheless, if an alternative title had to be chosen for *In Memoriam, Process and Reality* would do nicely.

29. C. F. G. Masterman, in his excellent study *Tennyson as a Religious Teacher* (1900; rpt. New York: Octagon, 1977), points out that Tennyson's Christianity consisted largely of admiration of its humanity and moral tone: "the doctrine of the Incarnation never took for him the great central position as the one supreme fact of history, beside which all else fades into insignificance. And consequently there was a certain tendency for it to disappear from his teaching: so that they are not altogether wrong who maintain that a vague theism is the only possible creed deductible from his later writings . . . He looked for the ideal man in man and never found the Christ (p. 210). H. N. Fairchild says much the same thing in *Religious Trends in English Poetry* (New York: Columbia University Press, 1957), 4:120–121. As an example of Tennyson's caution about—and sense of playfulness with—the Christian divinity, take the famous lines at the conclusion of *In Memoriam:* "That friend of mine who lives in God, / / That God, which ever lives and loves." Is the phrase "that God" a modification of the immediately preceding idea of "God," or is the whole second line rhetorical, parallel to and in apposition with the first, in which case Hallam has become God? Both interpretations are possible, and probably both were synonymous for Tennyson.

Six. The Various World: Tennyson's Epic Vision

1. The expression was originally R. J. Mann's, in his *Maud Vindicated* (London, 1856), an essay of which Tennyson was greatly appreciative. He adopted the term as his own.

2. The condemnation of Tennyson for having chosen a representational, and therefore moral, framework for his later poetry may properly be said to have begun with Swinburne. More recently, Paul de Man has put the case against the kind of poetic form Tennyson chose as succinctly as is possible: "All representational poetry is always also allegorical, whether it be aware of it or not, and the allegorical power of the language undermines and obscures the specific literal meaning of a representation open to understanding. But all allegorical poetry must contain a representational element that invites and allows for understanding, only to discover that the understanding it reaches is necessarily in error." *Blindness and Insight: Essays in the Rhetoric of Contemporary Criticism* (New York: Oxford University Press, 1971), p. 185. *The Idylls of the King*, a work revealing a consciousness of the dilemma stated by de Man, plays with properties of allegory for its own purposes.

3. *Memoir*, 1:396. On the metrics of *Maud*, see Edward Stokes, "The Metrics of *Maud*," *Victorian Poetry* 2(1964):97–110, which describes how the poem's effect is accomplished through a carefully controlled use of meters.

4. The line, of course, is Eliot's "I will show you fear in a handful of dust," an echo of Tennyson's "Dead, long dead,/Long dead!/ And my heart is a handful of dust,/And the wheels go over my head" (II, 239–242). Eliot imitates the metrical shifts and balances of *Maud*, as well as some of the language and the general neurotic perspective Tennyson captured through his refinement of the idyll form. For a fuller discussion of Eliot's debt to Tennyson (which Eliot himself was careful to obscure), see S. Musgrove, "Eliot and Tennyson," in *T. S. Eliot*, ed. Hugh Kenner (Englewood Cliffs, N.J.: Prentice-Hall, 1962), pp. 73–85.

5. Housman is quoted in R. W. Chambers, *Man's Unconquerable Mind: Studies of English Writers from Blake to A. E. Housman and W. P. Ker* (1939; rpt. New York: Haskell House, 1967), p. 371. W. E. Gladstone's review of the first four Idylls appeared in the *Quarterly Review* 212(1859):454–485. For Mallock's recipe, originally published in *"The Inspired Singer's Recipe Book*, by A. Newdigate Prizeman" (London, 1877), see Kenneth Hopkins, *The Poets Laureate*, 3d ed. (New York: Barnes and Noble, 1973), p. 164.

6. " 'I like Launcelot better than Arthur,' said Lizzie. 'So did the Queen,' replied Frank.' " *The Eustace Diamonds*, ch. 19. Trollope's novel contains several references to Tennyson's "romance," which is similar to his own.

7. Swinburne, *Under the Microscope* (London, 1872); the quotation is from the edition, *Swinburne Replies*, ed. Clyde K. Hyder (Syracuse, N.Y.: Syracuse University Press, 1966), p. 58. For an excellent approach to the *Idylls* purely as idyll see J. M. Gray, "A Study in Idyl: Tennyson's *Coming of Arthur*," *Renaissance and Modern Studies* 14(1969):111–150. Henry Kozicki argues that the *Idylls* have the organization of Dionysian drama, in "Tennyson's *Idylls of the King* as Tragic Drama," *Victorian Poetry* 4(1966): 15–20.

8. Tennyson to Edward Fitzgerald, in *Tennyson and His Friends*, p. 146. This remark would otherwise be inexplicable from a man who devoted so much of his life to researching the Arthurian tradition.

9. Allingham, *Diary*, pp. 156, 293.

10. Ibid., p. 331.

11. *Quarterly Review* 212 (1859), 469.

12. Allingham, *Diary*, p. 294.

13. *The Letters of Gerard Manley Hopkins and Richard Watson Dixon*, ed. C. C. Abbott (New York: Oxford University Press, 1955), p. 43.

14. Tennyson's copies of *La Gerusalemme liberata* were the Stamperia del Seminario edition (Pavdova, 1728), containing the

"Allegoria del poema" (this copy had been in his father's library at Lincoln); a 4-vol. Italian-language edition (Avignone, 1816); and Fairfax's translation, 5th ed. (Windsor, 1817). The copy of the Fairfax translation is inscribed "A.T. from R.J.T."—initials that fit only R. J. Tennant. If Tennant was the donor, the gift must have been made in the Cambridge years or shortly thereafter, for Tennyson and Tennant were not close friends after the early 1830s. See *Memoir,* 1:177. "The Allegory of the Poem," from which the quotations were taken, is on pp. v–xiii of the Fairfax translation.

15. Tennyson to Knowles, in *Tennyson and His Friends,* p. 498; Allingham, *Diary,* p. 150. John Rosenberg, in *The Fall of Camelot: A Study of Tennyson's Idylls of the King* (Cambridge: Harvard University Press, 1973), treats Tennyson's allegory in the proper spirit: "By 'parabolic drift' and 'thought within the image' Tennyson means precisely what we mean by *symbol,* the antithesis of the reductive, this-for-that equivalence which his commentators have found in the *Idylls*" (p. 22). Rosenberg argues that we should not call the method of the *Idylls* allegorical at all. I continue to do so because Tennyson did and because his method has clear links with the tradition of allegory, most notably that of the Italian poets of the Trecento and Renaissance. True, it evolves that tradition, using the idyll form as a catalyst, as Rosenberg points out: "Building on the techniques of the classical idyll, with its intensification of mood, its highly allusive texture, its startling juxapositions, flashbacks, and deliberate discontinuities, Tennyson creates an inclusive psychological landscape in which all the separate consciousnesses in the poem participate and in which each action is bound to all others through symbol, prophecy, or retrospect" (p. 27). This is the traditional ambition of all idyll; to stress it exclusively is in part to ignore formal components that Tennyson also wished to embrace in his *Idylls.*

16. *Tennyson and His Friends,* p. 498.

17. Tennyson, *The Ante-Chamber* (1834), ll.28–31.

Index

de Vere, Aubrey, 103, 140
Donne, John, 33, 158n
Drama, 14, 25–28, 113, 129, 132–133, 151
Dramatic monologue, history of, 17, 24–27, 32, 35, 156n, 157n; Tennyson's use of, 51–55, 89–91, 129, 131, 141

Elegiac poetry, 5, 30, 42, 103–108, 109–110, 125
Elegy, 17, 103–106, 109–110, 112, 120, 125, 127, 150
Eliot, T. S., 133, 170n
Epic, 5, 99, 112, 143–144; and its influence on idyll, 20–24, 27, 30–31, 34, 46, 93, 124; Tennyson's use of, 14, 46, 66–67, 93–94, 124, 134–135, 140–151
Epicharmus, 25, 27–28, 139
Epithalamium, 110–111, 119, 127
Epyllion, 17, 31–32, 47, 52
Euripedes, 26, 28

Fitzgerald, Edward, 61, 103; *Rubaiyat of Omar Khayyam*, 61–62
Forms of Poetry, *see* separate headings under names of various genres

Gibbon, Edward, 79–80
Gladstone, William Ewart, 134, 135, 140
Golden Treasury, The, 17
Gray, Thomas, 5, 123; *Elegy Written in a Country Churchyard*, 2, 34–35, 51, 105–106, 120
Guest, Charlotte, 136

Hallam, Arthur Henry, and *In Memoriam*, 103, 112–116, 118–120, 123–127, 167n; views on Tennyson's poetry, 11, 48–49, 113–115, 128–129
Heraclitus, 63, 116–118

Homer, 2, 5, 11, 20–24, 104, 140, 143; *Iliad*, 22, 106; *Odyssey*, 21–23, 84
Hopkins, Gerard Manley, 143
Horace, 8, 29, 33, 40–41
Housman, A. E., 134
Hugo, Victor, 113–114, 166n
Hyper-Doricism, 27

Idyll, definition and history of, 14–40; formal eclecticism in, 20–29; and *The Idylls of the King*, 135–140, 143–144, 146, 151; and *In Memoriam*, 103, 112, 113, 117–121, 128; and *Maud*, 129–130, 132–134; objectivity in, 18–20, 25–28, 35–36, 50, 62–63, 93; and psychology, 21–23, 31–32, 35, 49, 91, 93, 129, 132; and Tennyson's early poetry, 14–17, 22, 29, 40–63, 64–92. *See also* Dramatic monologue; Pastoral; Tennyson, *English Idyls*

Juvenal, 33, 79

Keats, John, 8–9, 14, 20, 38, 45, 46, 154n; *Endymion*, 36; *Eve of St. Agnes*, 8; *Isabella*, 8–9; *Sleep and Poetry*, 8
Knowles, James, 108, 145

Landor, Walter Savage, 16
Livy, 31
Lushington, Edmund, 110–111
Lyell, Charles, *Principles of Geology*, 112
Lyric, 17; and the idyllic tradition, 22, 24–25, 29, 35, 37 49; in *Idylls of the King*, 142–143, 147, 148; in *In Memoriam*, 103, 111–112, 120–124, 128, 129; in *Maud*, 129, 132–134; in *The Princess*, 99–102; in Tennyson's early poetry, 10–11, 14, 40–41, 49; Tennyson's suspicion of, 41, 100, 123, 142